Elite • 152

The British Reconnaissance Corps in World War II

Richard Doherty • Illustrated by Rob Chapman

Consultant editor Martin Windrow

First published in Great Britain in 2007 by Osprey Publishing,
Midland House, West Way, Botley, Oxford OX2 0PH, UK
443 Park Avenue South, New York, NY 10016, USA

Email: info@ospreypublishing.com

ISBN 978 1 84603 122 9

Editor: Martin Windrow
Page layouts by Ken Vail Graphic Design, Cambridge, UK
Typeset in Helvetica Neue and ITC New Baskerville
Index by Glyn Sutcliffe
Originated by PPS Grasmere, Leeds, UK
Printed in China through World Print Ltd.

07 08 09 10 11   10 9 8 7 6 5 4 3 2 1

A CIP catalogue record for this book
is available from the British Library

FOR A CATALOGUE OF ALL BOOKS PUBLISHED BY
OSPREY MILITARY AND AVIATION PLEASE CONTACT:

North America:
Osprey Direct
C/o Random House Distribution Centre, 400 Hahn Road, Westminster,
MD 21157, USA
Email: info@ospreydirect.com

All other regions:
Osprey Direct UK
PO Box 140, Wellingborough, Northants, NN8 2FA, UK
Email: info@ospreydirect.co.uk

Buy online at www.ospreypublishing.com

Dedication

To all who served in the Reconnaissance Corps, and
especially to those who lost their lives in that service.
When 4 Recce was disbanded in Greece in 1945, one
of that unit's soldiers wrote a tribute to his regiment
that may stand for the whole Corps:

> *Now strike the flag, the panther green and gold,*
> *That for four years has fluttered to the sky*
> *In seven countries; fold the colours now,*
> *They are not needed, fold them, lay them by.*

Acknowledgements

Thanks are due to the many people who helped with this
book by providing information or photographs. Their
enthusiasm for the Reconnaissance Corps is clear, and
hopefully this book will be worthy of their support and
encouragement.

Artist's Note

Readers may care to note that the original paintings from
which the colour plates in this book were prepared are
available for private sale. All reproduction copyright
whatsoever is retained by the Publishers. All enquiries
should be addressed to:

Rob Chapman,
Old Furnace Cottage,
Greendale,
Oakamoor,
Staffordshre
ST10 3AP, UK

The Publishers regret that they can enter into no
correspondence upon this matter.

RECONNAISSANCE CORPS IN WORLD WAR II

BACKGROUND

British experience early in World War II led to many new regiments and corps being added to the Army List; and it was analysis of the performance of the British Expeditionary Force (BEF) in France in 1940 – by a committee under MajGen Bartholomew – that led to the creation of the Reconnaissance Corps. Among the committee's findings was that there were insufficient cavalry regiments to perform the traditional role of reconnaissance for major formations other than the armoured divisions. After considering several means of providing reconnaissance for infantry divisions, the final decision was to create an Infantry Reconnaissance Corps. This new corps – in the event styled simply the Reconnaissance Corps – was born on 14 January 1941 under Royal Warrant, and the War Office published a Special Army Order eight days later (However, several Reconnaissance units are shown as having come into being on 8 January, with at least one dating its inception to 1 January in its war diary.)

Initially the Corps adopted infantry nomenclature, with all units numbered as battalions, of which there were to be 12 – one for each operational army corps; it was considered impractical to provide one for each division immediately. Most battalions were created in one of two ways. Some were infantry battalions converted to the reconnaissance role, including 4th and 8th Royal Northumberland Fusiliers, 5th and 6th Loyals (North Lancs), 21st Royal Fusiliers, 5th Glosters, and 3rd Tower Hamlets Rifles from the Rifle Brigade. Others were created from brigade anti-tank companies, many of which had been re-roled as brigade reconnaissance groups in the 'higher establishment' divisions – those intended to deploy with field armies. In the 'lower establishment' divisions, independent reconnaissance companies were to be formed for each brigade; some of these companies would later amalgamate to form additional units of the Corps.

After many submissions for a Corps badge had been rejected, the final choice came down to a design submitted by 56th Bn; created by Tpr George Jones, a commercial artist in civilian life, this showed an upwards-pointing spear flanked by two lightning bolts. With the addition of a scroll reading 'Reconnaissance Corps' this design was adopted on 29 July 1941,

gold.

Whistler also submitted these designs including a stylized compass rose; one incorporates the letter 'R' with the four principal bearings and the old Army scout's fleur-de-lys badge, and the other the 'ever-open eye' of the Guards Division. Whistler's company did not remain long with the Corps, since the Guards refused to allow their personnel to transfer to it. The artist was later killed on active service in Normandy in summer 1944 when serving with 2nd Bn Welsh Guards, the reconnaissance unit of Guards Armoured Division. (NA WO32/4720)

although the first badges were not issued until September due to the manufacturer's premises being damaged by German bombing. By the end of 1941 an officer's version, with gilt spear and nickel-plated lightnings and title, had been introduced. (See Plate H for these and other insignia details.) Since the reconnaissance role had, by tradition, been discharged by cavalry units, it was no surprise that the infantrymen of the Reconnaissance Corps began adopting a cavalry culture. This led to several battalions styling themselves 'regiments' and using cavalry nomenclature: private soldiers became troopers, companies became squadrons and platoons became troops (at least one unit even purchased cavalry trumpets to replace their bugles). On 6 June 1942 the War Office accepted this practice, and cavalry terms became official; from that date, battalions became 'regiments' of the Corps.

TRAINING & EQUIPMENT

The Reconnaissance Corps was charged with gathering 'vital tactical information in battle for infantry divisions'. The Training Centre was established at Winchester on 1 February 1941; with the expansion of the Corps other centres were established at Lochmaben, Dumfriesshire (No.1), and Scarborough, Yorkshire (No.2), with a Tactical Training School at Annan close to No.1 Training Centre. Eventually, the home of the Corps moved to Catterick in Yorkshire. Through this training structure, plus recommendations from units in action, the Corps developed its operational practices. As early as April 1941 one unit

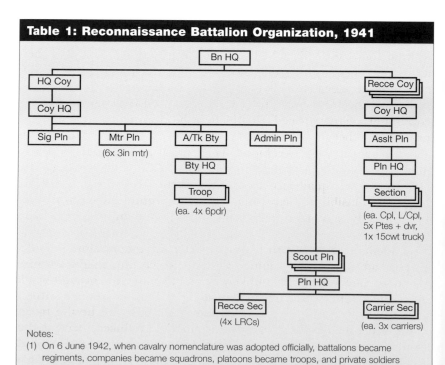

Table 1: Reconnaissance Battalion Organization, 1941

Bn HQ

HQ Coy — Coy HQ — Sig Pln, Mtr Pln (6x 3in mtr), A/Tk Bty — Bty HQ — Troop (ea. 4x 6pdr), Admin Pln

Recce Coy — Coy HQ — Asslt Pln — Pln HQ — Section (ea. Cpl, L/Cpl, 5x Ptes + dvr, 1x 15cwt truck)

Scout Pln — Pln HQ — Recce Sec (4x LRCs), Carrier Sec (ea. 3x carriers)

Notes:
(1) On 6 June 1942, when cavalry nomenclature was adopted officially, battalions became regiments, companies became squadrons, platoons became troops, and private soldiers became troopers.
(2) As a result of experience in Tunisia, armoured cars were issued to regiments; each **recce section** then deployed 2x 'heavy' armoured cars (HACs) and 3x light recce cars (LRCs).

was suggesting changes in the war establishment of a battalion, as well as the replacement of No.18 radio sets, used for communication between company and platoon, with the No.11 set. Changes to the numbers and types of vehicles used were also suggested.

In its formative months the Corps was well down the War Office priority list for weapons and equipment; units often had to improvise, but this was no deterrent to men expected to display initiative and quick thinking in action. The results were seen in some of the early vehicles used by battalions. Reconnoitring on the battlefield required a high degree of mobility which, in turn, called for many more drivers and mechanics than in a standard infantry unit. Relaying information demanded skilled wireless operators, and men to maintain their sets. Sir Arthur Bryant summarized the role of the Corps as being that of 'the cat's whiskers – armoured, mechanized, transmitting whiskers. Those who served had to be intelligent, enterprising, brave, enduring and highly skilled'.

Indeed, the public were given an impression of super soldiers. The *Daily Mail* described Recce men as 'tough with cold, scientific brains behind their brawn'. Some press reports even suggested that the Corps might make the Commandos redundant, since its soldiers could march scores of miles in a day, without food, and still fight like furies. Even within the Corps there was some uncertainty over how it should function. One divisional commander declared that a Recce battalion had two roles: reconnaissance and protection, which required different tactics and could not be performed simultaneously. Fortunately the training programme began to remove such uncertainties as sound tactics and procedures were developed. The TTS at Annan was particularly important; it was there that officers and NCOs studied the tactical deployment of squadrons, troops and sections. Junior officers had more responsibility than their infantry counterparts, and were supported by a higher proportion of NCOs than in an ordinary infantry battalion.

Students at Annan also learned of the three conditions – coded green, amber and red – under which a Recce unit might advance. Where enemy forces were unlikely to be encountered the unit would 'move in green', travelling quickly along its axis of advance without searching the surrounding countryside. If contact with hostile troops was possible then the unit 'moved in amber', at reduced speed so that scout cars could do some searching by detouring along sideroads and tracks off the main axis. Where the enemy was known to be present the unit would 'move in red': close reconnaissance was necessary, speed was reduced considerably, and everyone was prepared for immediate action.

By Appointment to H.M. The King

J. R. GAUNT & SON Ltd.

INFANTRY RECONNAISSANCE CORPS

O.5146

MEDALLISTS & BADGE MAKERS
LONDON & BIRMINGHAM.
Established 200 Years.

A number of designs for a Corps badge were submitted by the manufacturers J.R.Gaunt & Son, including this pointer dog, rejected because it might have led to the nickname 'Dogsbodies'. It was claimed that another, featuring a leopard, would be mistaken for a cheetah and would encourage the nickname 'Cheaters'; and one with a hawk was turned down to avoid confusion with that of the Army Air Corps. (NA WO32/4720)

Both the vehicles and the weapons that the Corps needed to perform its duties were in short supply in 1941, and improvisation led to the development of vehicles suitable for training but not for action. These included the Beaverette, a four-wheeled car fitted with light armour plating and armed with a Bren gun. Bedford 30cwt lorries armoured with boilerplate and known as 'Ironsides' were pressed into service; the name Ironside was also applied to the Humber Mk I Light Reconnaissance Car (LRC), built on the chassis of a Humber Snipe saloon. These interim vehicles gave way to the Humber Mk II LRC, a two-wheel-drive vehicle that was subsequently modified to have four-wheel drive. The first 4x4 LRCs, designated as Humber Mk III LRCs, were issued to 4 Recce on 6 January 1942.

While the Corps waited for proper vehicles, improvised machines such as this Beaverette III were used. Built by the Standard Car Co, this lightly armoured saloon fitted with a Bren LMG was termed the 'Standard Car 4x2' in the Army, and the 'Car, Armoured, Light Standard Type C Beaverette I' in the RAF, which used it for airfield defence. (IWM H 14875)

During the early days of public confusion over the Corps' role, it was probably this press photograph that inspired the BBC to suggest that Recce soldiers would throw themselves down on barbed-wire barriers to allow infantry to run over them – an image that owed more to the Great War than to modern mobile warfare. (Imperial War Museum H 28088)

Table 2: Reconnaissance unit basic equipment

	Recce Bn, 1941	Recce Regt, 1942
Humber LRCs	45 (later, 52)	45 (later, + HACs)
Cars, 4-seater	5	6 (usually Humber staff cars)
Carriers	67	67
Trucks, 15 cwt	69	71
(42x GS, 4x wireless, 23x personnel)		
Lorries, 3 ton	6	6
Motorcycles	71	71
Bren guns	126	126
Bren guns, twin, AA	4	4
AT rifles, .55in	48 (later, 2pdr/ 6pdr AI guns & PIATs)	
2in mortars	18	18
3in mortars	2	2 (later, 6x)
Wireless sets No.18	12 + 2 spares	12 + 2
(comms Sqn HQs/ Troops)		
Wireless sets No.11	4 + 1 spare	4 + 1
(comms Sqn HQs/ RHQ; each in 1x 15cwt truck)		
Wireless set No.9	1	1
(in attached Div sigs secn; comms RHQ/ Div HQ)		

Notes:
(1) In Jan 1941, small arms were listed as 95x .38in pistols (later, 40x); 12x .45in Thompson SMGs (later, 9mm Stens); 675x .303in rifles; 180x grenades; and 30x signal pistols
(2) There were other vehicles in the regimental inventory, such as water tankers etc. The body text and photos show the variety of LRCs & HACs in use. 52 (Lowland) Recce initially had a Valentine tank squadron, and kept Daimler Dingo scout cars; 6 Abn Armd Recce used Tetrarch & Locust light tanks and jeeps.

These Gaunt proposals were also rejected – because the ferret might have caused 'a lot of noisome discussion'; because the Colonel of the Manchester Regt might have objected to the close likeness between the wreathed fleur-de-lys and the badge of his own regiment; and because the Indian-head was felt to be un-British. (NA WO32/4720)

In the course of the war the LRC would be supplemented with or replaced by other vehicles, both British and American, and armoured cars – again, both British and American – were added to regimental inventories. Several units had a different line-up of vehicles; these included the two airborne units – 1st Abn Sqn, which had motorcycles and jeeps, and 6th Abn Armd Regt, which had two troops of Tetrarch and later Locust light tanks. 52 (Lowland) Recce for a time deployed a squadron of Valentine tanks, and also relied heavily on the Dingo scout car – the only Corps unit to do so. This regiment was part of 52nd (Lowland) Div, which trained for mountain warfare before becoming – theoretically – an air-portable formation.

The Universal ('Bren gun') carrier was employed by Recce units at regimental and squadron HQ level as well as in the reconnaissance squadrons (see Table 1). Motorcycles, light trucks and lorries were also included among unit vehicles. Each of the three recce squadrons in a regiment deployed three recce troops and one infantry or assault troop, the latter using a 15cwt truck for each of its three sections and another two in troop HQ; 71 of these trucks were allocated to each regiment.

Such a range of vehicles allowed Recce units to deploy with considerable mobility and speed, but they also packed a punch. While total regimental manpower, including attached specialists, was 770 men – not much larger than the standard early-war infantry battalion – the firepower was considerably greater (see Table 2). With this variety of vehicles, weapons and communications equipment, it was clear that the recce soldier, although an infantryman, needed a wider than normal range of

Other improvised AFVs included these 'Ironsides' of 15 (Scottish) Recce, which were based on Bedford 30-cwt lorries. (Sir John Boynton)

skills. In addition to skill-at-arms, fieldcraft and map-reading, he might also have to be a driver, mechanic or radio operator (see Table 3). Recce soldiers were subjected to an IQ test to determine their suitability; many failed and were transferred to infantry battalions, but those who succeeded enjoyed the kudos of belonging to an elite organization, and were determined to prove their worth.

Units

A summary of all Reconnaissance Corps units will be found in Table 6 on page 52.

On 1 January 1944, the Corps was officially absorbed into the Royal Armoured Corps, its regiments being styled thereafter as e.g. 4th Reconnaissance Regiment, RAC. (This should have brought an immediate change from the Reconnaissance Corps' khaki beret to the black of the RAC; in fact individual units took their time, and it was to be spring 1945 before the last regiments complied.)

The iconic vehicle of the Reconnaissance Corps, straight from the factory: the Humber LRC had a three-man crew and featured a small open-topped turret, a .55-inch Boys AT rifle, a Bren LMG and a smoke mortar, and carried a No.19 wireless set. The 26.88hp engine gave the 3.6-ton LRC a top speed of 61mph, and its 18gal fuel tank a range of 175 miles. Another contender for the LRC role was a vehicle produced by the Morris Motor Co, but no Morris LRCs saw active service. (IWM MH 3748)

INTO ACTION: NORTH AFRICA

The very first unit of the Corps to see action – although not in its intended role – was 18th Bn, formerly 5th Bn The Loyal Regt (North Lancs). This left the UK on 22 October 1941, destined for North Africa with 18th (East Anglian) Division. However, while the division was at sea the Japanese attacked in the Far East, and 18th Div was diverted via India to Singapore to join III Indian Corps. The battalion was destroyed in the fall of Singapore in February 1942 (see below, 'The Far East').

By the end of April 1942, 50th Bn had deployed to join 22 Armd Bde on the Gazala Line in Libya, where Eighth Army was preparing for an offensive. At the end of May, however, the Panzer Armee Afrika struck first, and the three defensive 'boxes' held by that brigade – each including one company of 50 Recce – came under repeated attack over several days. All three 'boxes' were finally overrun, and 50 Recce's CO, LtCol E.P.A.des Graz, was killed while manning an anti-tank gun. Most unit personnel were taken prisoner as Rommel swept on towards Tobruk. The battalion was not re-formed, and its place as the 'eyes' of 50th (Northumbrian) Div was later taken by 61 Recce.

The fate of 50 Recce probably influenced LtGen Montgomery – GOC Eighth Army from August 1942 – to declare that he saw no role for such units in the desert. Thus 44th and 51st Reconnaissance Regts were both to fight in roles for which they had never been intended; that they did so successfully proved the adaptability of the Corps.

The former, reorganized as 44th Divisional Reconnaissance Carrier Regt and including Royal Engineers, carried out the dangerous task of clearing gaps through the 'January' and 'February' minefields in front of 7th Armd Div on Eighth Army's southern flank for the opening of the El Alamein offensive on 23 October 1942. The unit lost more than 100 officers and men killed or wounded, and only four of its 38 carriers survived. The regiment later took part in the pursuit of Panzer Armee Afrika, but was due to be disbanded, along with its parent 44th

The Universal ('Bren gun') carrier remained a stalwart of the Corps throughout the war. Each of a regiment's recce squadrons had a carrier in SHQ and another in each of the recce troop HQs, and each recce troop deployed two carrier sections each with three vehicles. In this scene from an early exercise, Beaverette IIs and motorcycles can also be seen in the background. (Author's collection)

A carefully arranged press shot showing a pristine Humber LRC in a 'warlike' pose; the neatly parked motorcycles on the left are a giveaway. The unit is unidentified, but the St Andrew's Cross suggests 52 (Lowland) Recce. (Tank Museum 2077/C4)

(Home Counties) Div when it was reprieved and, re-equipped with Marmon-Herrington armoured cars, was subsequently assigned to 56th (London) Div, which had arrived in the Middle East without its reconnaissance regiment.

Between disembarking in Egypt and joining Eighth Army, 51 (Highland) Recce formed part of Delta Force to defend Cairo against the possibility of attack. Before El Alamein it was reorganized into two squadrons – a 'Composite' and an 'Infantry' or assault squadron. The latter was intended to protect Sappers creating gaps through the northern minefields and, once again, the squadron's carriers proved easy targets for Axis AT guns. Before being withdrawn into reserve the Composite Sqn took part in the assault on objective 'Nairn', at a cost of some 70 killed or wounded. The squadron then performed a normal recce role for 51st (Highland) Div in its advance to Fuka, where the regiment reverted to conventional form – only to be ordered back to Cairo for conversion into a motorized infantry unit, as 14th Bn, Highland Light Infantry.

* * *

As Eighth Army pursued the Panzer Armee westwards 'up the desert', First Army was landing in French North Africa in Operation 'Torch', in the hope that a race for Tunis would trap Axis forces by a pincer movement. The leading element, Bladeforce, included a squadron of

56 Recce – which would be nicknamed 'Chavasse's Light Horse', in honour of its CO, LtCol Kendal Chavasse. Originally the recce battalion of 56th (London) Div, the regiment had been transferred to the 78th Div in September 1942.

Elements of 56 Recce were probably the first Allied troops into Tunisia and, before long, their carriers and LRCs found themselves up against heavy armoured cars and tanks. Among its first soldiers decorated for gallantry was Sgt Crutch of C Sqn, who used his carrier to butt aside a damaged Panzer that had been dumped as a roadblock, before approaching close to the enemy and bringing back accurate information on their dispositions. Shortly afterwards the regiment was assigned to protect 78th Div's right flank as the push for Tunis continued. In spite of bad weather and fierce opposition on the ground and from the air, 56 Recce advanced to within 15 miles of Tunis by early December; but the Allied advance ground to a stop by the 10th. Among the tasks falling to 56 Recce during December was the rescue of men of 2nd Parachute Bn who had been cut off in the Sloughia area.

The Corps first saw action in its true role in Tunisia. Here carriers of an unidentified recce regiment move 'in red' across the Tunisian countryside; in the foreground, a Boys AT rifle has been lifted on to the top edge of the gunner's armour. (IWM NA 885)

During the major Axis offensive in February 1943, A Sqn of 56 Recce was deployed to support US troops in the fighting around Kasserine Pass. By now 56 Recce had been joined in Tunisia by 46 Recce. Both units were engaged around El Aroussa while 'Ochsenkopf' – the second phase of the Axis offensive – was beaten back. Late in the month 56 Recce was responsible for the survival of No.6 Commando, an action that brought a letter of thanks to LtCol Chavasse from Lord Louis Mountbatten, head of Combined Operations. No one was surprised when Chavasse was awarded the DSO for his inspiring leadership; among other episodes, he personally led a seven-hour carrier patrol, with LtCol Mills-Roberts of No.6 Commando acting as the gunner in his carrier.

By April 1943, 56 and 46 Recce had been joined by further Reconnaissance Corps units; in order of arrival these were 1 Recce, 4 Recce and 44 Recce. While the others were shipped in to join First Army, 44 Recce arrived overland from the south-east with Eighth Army's advance, assigned to 56th (London) Division.

Having briefly relieved 56 Recce at the front in early February, by the end of that month 46 Recce deployed its A Sqn to Hunt's Gap during 'Ochsenkopf'. There it saw action over several days; meanwhile B Sqn was also engaged, liaising with a squadron of 56 Recce and observing enemy movement in the Dr Bed valley. Fighting continued into March, with B Sqn working alongside 56 Recce; A Sqn provided

Table 3: Establishment of a Reconnaissance Regiment, from August 1942

RHQ
(Personnel) Commanding Officer (LtCol), 2nd in command (Maj), Adjutant (Capt), Intelligence Officer (IO, Capt/ Lt), Medical Officer (RMO); RSM, Provost Sgt, Intel Sgt, Orderly Room Sgt + 2x clerks, 6x Intel troopers, 2x driver/mechanics, 3x drivers, RMO's orderly, 3x batmen
(Vehicles) 3x LRCs (CO, 2ic, IO), 7x motorcycles, 3x trucks 15cwt 4x4

HQ Squadron:
Sqn HQ
(P) Sqn leader (Maj), 2ic (Capt), SSM, clerk, dvr/mech, batman
(V) 1x jeep, 1x car 4-seater

Anti-aircraft Troop
(P) Sgt, Cpl, 2x gun numbers, dvr
(V) 2x trucks 15cwt, 1x m'cycle

Signal Troop
(P) Tp ldr (Lt), Sgt M'cycle Secn, Cpl M'cycle Secn, 19x orderlies, Sgt Sigs Secn, 3x dvr/operators, dvr, batman
(V) 1x truck 15cwt wireless, 1x truck 15cwt GS, 23x m'cycles

Mortar Troop
(P) Tp ldr (Lt), 3x Secn Sgts, 3x Carrier Sgts, 5x mortar numbers, dvr/mech, dvr, batman
(V) 1x jeep, 1x truck 15cwt personnel, 2x carriers, 1x m'cycle

Anti-tank Troop HQ
(P) Tp cdr (Capt), 2ic (Lt), Tp Sgt, batman
(V) 1x jeep, 2x m'cycles

3x AT Sections
(P) 3x Sgts, 3x L/Sgts, 3x Cpls, 10x gun numbers, 3x dvr/mechs, 3x orderlies, 3x fitters, dvr
(V) 3x Lloyd carriers, 3x trucks 15cwt 4x4 personnel, 3x m'cycles

Administrative Troop
(P) Quartermaster (Maj/Capt), Technical Officer (Capt), Transport Officer (Lt), RQMS, SQMS, Fitter Staff Sgt, Trspt Sgt, armourer

(RAOC), 3x cooks, 2x clerks, 3x dvr/mechs, 2x motor mechs, 3x tech storemen, 2x storemen, 5x dvrs, butchery dutyman, sanitary dutyman, water dutyman, carpenter/joiner, shoemaker, equpt repairer, armourer, postman, 3x batmen
(V) 3x lorries 3 ton, 2x trucks 15cwt personnel, 1x truck 15cwt 4x4 personnel, 1x truck 15cwt GS, 1x truck 15cwt water, 1x jeep, 3x m'cycles

3x Recce Squadrons, each:
Sqn HQ
(P) Sqn ldr (Maj), 2ic (Capt), SSM, SQMS, Trspt Cpl, 4x dvr/optrs, 2x dvr/mechs, 8x dvrs, 4x cooks, clerk, 2x batmen, 2x medical orderlies, carpenter/joiner, motor mech, storeman, tech stmn, sanitary dutyman, water dutyman, fitter, orderly
(V) 1x LRC, 1x jeep, 4x trucks 15cwt 4x4 personnel, 4x trucks 15cwt GS, 1x lorry 3 ton + water trailer

Scout Troop HQ (3 per Recce Sqn), each:
(P) Tp ldr (Lt), Sgt, orderly, dvr/optr, dvr/mech
(V) 1x carrier, 2x m'cycles

Recce Section (1 per Scout Troop)
(P) Secn ldr car cmdr (Lt/2Lt), 3x dvr/optrs, 3x dvr/mechs, 2x dvrs, Sgt car cdr, 2x Cpl car cmdrs, L/Cpl car cmdr, trooper, batman
(V) 3x LRCs, 2x HACs

Carrier Section (2 per Scout Troop), each:
(P) Sgt, 3x Cpls, 3x dvr/mechs, 2x troopers
(V) 3x carriers

Assault Troop (1 per Recce Sqn)
(P) Tp ldr (Lt/2Lt), Sgt, orderly, batman, 5x Cpls, 4x dvrs, dvr/optr, dvr/mech, 26x troopers
(V) 1x jeep, 5x trucks 15cwt 4x4 personnel, 2x m'cycles

support and communications for two cut-off battalions of the Hampshire Regt from 46th Div's 128 Inf Bde – the squadron's assault troop was under constant mortar fire for 36 hours and suffered several casualties. 46 Recce's A Sqn was then tasked with keeping open the road between Beja, Chemical Corner and Khanguet Mine, while B Sqn co-ordinated a recce in force by 3rd Bn Grenadier Guards.

The CO of 46 Recce, LtCol F.H.Cotton, decided that offensive action was needed, since 'the enemy's policy has been gradual encroachment on to all dominating features, however insignificant, so that suddenly one wakes up to find him sitting on a feature dominating some vital position or line of communication below'. Cotton's advice was heeded, and his C Sqn was augmented with two ad-hoc companies from the Durham Light Infantry, which provided the manpower to dominate the area. Intensive patrolling and support for other units – including 1 Parachute Bde – filled much of the remainder of March. C Squadron operated with a mixed force of British and French Colonial troops advancing to Sedjenane, taking prisoners and forcing the enemy back up the Sedjenane Valley to their former positions on Bald and Green Hills.

While 46 Recce carried out 'active patrolling' during early April, 56 Recce took part in a 78th Div attack that captured Jebel el Nahel, Jebel el Mahdi and Mergued Chaouch. The regiment's C Sqn, operating with 11 Inf Bde, took about 100 prisoners; but the progress of A Sqn in the Dr Bed Valley was impeded by mines and by the loss of an alternative track which had been churned up by Churchill tanks. Pushing forward, A Sqn was later pinned down by heavy machine-gun and mortar fire and suffered several casualties, including the squadron leader and three of

13

his men killed. Lieutenant-Colonel Chavasse withdrew the squadron until the infantry could stabilize the situation, and before long A Sqn was once again making good progress. The following day B Sqn suffered a similar experience in much the same area, but by noon on 10 April the RHQ was established in the Dr Bed Valley.

The regiment went into divisional mobile reserve as 78th Div prepared to assault Jebel Tanngoucha. This phrase is misleading: the role entailed providing observation posts (OPs), flank guards and recce patrols, as well as soldiers to serve as infantry. 56 Recce was actively engaged, and by 25 April all divisional objectives had been taken. Squadrons of 56 Recce supported the three brigades of 78th Div as they fought their way forward in the final advance on Tunis itself.

In these battles of late April, 46 Recce was also committed heavily, working with B Sqn, 1st Derbyshire Yeomanry – the recce regiment of 6th Armd Div – to provide protection for 138 Inf Bde and French units. At the beginning of May the regiment, with 139 Inf Bde, came under command of 1st Armd Div to carry out patrolling and man OPs.

When 1 Recce arrived at the front in late March 1943 they too carried out a range of duties in support of British, French and US troops. On Banana Ridge the regiment lost its CO wounded; he was succeeded by Maj Paddy Brett. Although victory was now in sight there were still many determined German counter-attacks; one such occurred at Gab Gab Gap, where elements of 1 Recce fought several desperate actions. One regimental OP directed artillery fire, while Sgt Harry Salt

The Marmon-Herrington armoured car also saw some service with the Corps; it was used by 44 Recce, and also by 5 Recce, which had served in Persia and Palestine before joining Eighth Army for the invasion of Sicily. This is a 'sawn-off' car fitted with a 47mm gun. (Tank Museum 636/F3)

with men of 13 Tp, alongside Irish Guardsmen, fought off three German attempts to take Point 212. Salt was killed the following day, and the Irish Guards spoke highly of his leadership and courage; many believed that his actions merited the Victoria Cross, but no award was ever made. In the closing days of the campaign 1 Recce supported 4th Indian Div until the final Axis surrender on 12 May.

Also involved in the final phase was 4 Recce, who first went into action near Sidi Nsir in early April; linking up with 46 Recce, they carried out many patrols. Relieved by US troops, 4th Div redeployed for the final attacks; but the Germans then struck at Banana Ridge, Grenadier Hill and Jebel Jaffa, and 4 Recce was heavily engaged. When the Allied Operation 'Vulcan' began, 4 Recce's squadrons deployed with the division's infantry brigades. When the Allies finally broke through, A Sqn's leading troop began a sweep northward around the Cape Bon peninsula on 11 May, and was soon taking many prisoners. As the day wore on B Sqn also pushed into the peninsula; and in the dying hours of the campaign its Sgt Don Smith earned an immediate Military Medal when he saved the crew of an armoured car that had been knocked out by a Panzer. 'Smudger' Smith, with seven men, held back four lorry loads of enemy infantry as the wounded were taken to safety. The arrival of 'heavy' armoured cars (HACs) also marked an addition to the equipment of reconnaissance regiments, following a recommendation from LtCol Chavasse of 56 Recce. The only recce unit with Eighth Army, 44 Recce, arrived at Enfidaville on 24 April. Although it saw little combat compared to its sister regiments, it spent much time on the receiving end of German

At the end of the Tunisian campaign several members of 56 Recce, the first unit to see action in the true reconnaissance role, were decorated for their service. This group from 'Chavasse's Light Horse' includes (third from right) the CO, LtCol Kendal Chavasse, who was awarded the DSO (see Plates C3 & D1). Note the contrasting shades of the berets – khaki for the three other ranks on the left, and green for the three officers on the right. (Author's collection, via 56 Recce OCA)

A line-up of HQ Sqn LRCs of 56 Recce in Tunisia; second from right is the CO's car, 'Faugh A Ballagh' – see Plate E1. The other cars display the old British armoured recognition flash of red/white/red stripes immediately right of the driver's visor (as viewed). The right hand car also bears a Gaelic name – LtCol Chavasse's second-in-command was also an Irishman. (Author's collection, via 56 Recce OCA)

artillery fire. Patrols from 44 Recce engaged enemy troops, repulsed several attacks and captured prisoners; and it was a patrol from 44 Recce that made Eighth Army's first contact with soldiers of First Army, pushing down from the north.

THE MEDITERRANEAN

Sicily

From the first landings on 10 July until the skilful German evacuation at Messina the campaign lasted just 39 days, with only two recce regiments involved. Among the assault divisions for Operation 'Husky' was 5th Div, and 5 Recce mopped up Italian resistance near Augusta on 14 July. Before long the unit was facing stiffer opposition. They also learned that reconnaissance units had, at times, to fight as conventional infantry; they held part of the line with the spirit to be expected from Riflemen – this regiment had its origins as 3rd Bn Tower Hamlets Rifles, a Territorial unit of the Rifle Brigade. 56 Recce landed later in July with 78th Division. Although the topography of Sicily was not ideal for reconnaissance regiments, both 5 and 56 Recce carried out effectively every task assigned to them.

Italy

The invasion of Italy began on 3 September 1943 with Eighth Army's landings in the 'toe' of the Calabrian peninsula, followed by the Anglo-American assault at Salerno on the west coast six days later. Recce units were early into action, with 5 Recce probing in front of the advance through Calabria, and 44 and 46 Recce landing at Salerno. Additional elements of Eighth Army landed in the south-east at Taranto, from where 1st Air-Landing Recce Sqn from 1st Airborne Div struck out to the

Adriatic coast. The squadron was soon withdrawn to the UK with the other Airborne units; it would next see action at Arnhem. 56 Recce also arrived through Taranto with 78th Division.

At Salerno, elements of both 44 and 46 Recce were among the first troops of their divisions to land, and found themselves holding the line as the Germans tried to push the Allies back into the sea. Eventually the beachhead was secured, and these regiments were able to reconnoitre for 56th and 46th Divs as X Corps advanced on Naples. However, Field Marshal Kesselring's determined and skilful defensive campaigns in Italy have passed into the textbooks; and in winter 1943/44 the Allied advance ran into the mountain defences of the Gustav Line, which would not be broken until May 1944. During that first winter, 44 and 46 Recce were assigned a wide range of duties, working with artillery, engineers, infantry and light armoured units.

During the struggle for Monte Camino in the first half of November much of 44 Recce was employed portering supplies up to 167 Bde's infantry, while other elements carried out patrols. Captain Osmond of A Sqn spent two days behind enemy lines, on a patrol described as 'an inspiration to every officer in the division' by the GOC, MajGen Gerald Templer. Osmond repeated the performance some days later, and also

When the forces besieged in the Anzio beachhead broke out at the end of May 1944, the first junction with the main body of US Fifth Army punching up from the south was made by a Recce officer, Lt R.G.A.Beale, MC, of 1 Recce; he is seen with Lt Leroy R.Weil of Chicago. Beale displays no insignia apart from the Corps cap badge, shoulder title and rank badges; his ribbons are the Military Cross, and the Africa Star with First Army '1'. (IWM NA 15402)

Self-propelled 75mm guns of a Recce unit – possibly those of 4 Recce – in action during the Operation 'Olive' battles, to break through the eastern or Adriatic sector of the Gothic Line, in August/September 1944. These are old US 75mm GMC M3 tank-destroyers – outdated in that role, but still providing useful all-purpose mobile supporting fire for a number of Allied motorized and infantry units. (Tank Museum 2986/E6)

single-handedly cleared a dozen Germans from Colle. When 56th Div launched its attack on Monte Camino the soldiers of 44 Recce attacked alongside the infantry companies for which they were portering. The regiment remained facing the Gustav Line until withdrawn to Egypt in May 1944, just before the final successful offensive that broke into the Liri Valley.

The troopers of 46 Recce also endured all the rigours of winter fighting in the hills. From its landing in September 1943 until 29 February 1944, 46 Recce was in constant action; B Sqn spent a period of eight weeks in the line with only a two-day break.

Further to the east, 56 Recce had led Eighth Army's advance on the Foggia Plain and then made for Termoli on the Adriatic coast, where it was hoped to outflank the Germans through a seaborne landing combined with an advance led by 56 Recce; elements of 78th Div were involved in both parts of the operation. However, Termoli was then attacked by 16. Panzer Division and, with torrential rain delaying the arrival of reinforcements and grounding Allied aircraft, an ad hoc group commanded by LtCol Chavasse was assigned to defend the perimeter. This force included commandos and a Special Raiding Sqn troop, as well as a squadron from 56 Recce and some infantry. Chavasse's small command held off the enemy long enough for reinforcements to arrive by both road and sea; for this action Chavasse received a Bar (second award) to his DSO. One of the recce soldiers who fell during this battle was Tpr Alfred Ives, while manning an anti-tank gun in the face of attacking Panzer IVs.

1944

In an effort to draw German defenders from the Gustav Line, the Anglo-American VI Corps of US Fifth Army was landed behind their right shoulders at Anzio, south of Rome, on 22 January 1944. This corps included the British 1st Div; but instead of reconnoitring inland through the Alban Hills, 1 Recce soon found itself besieged in the beachhead with the rest of the landing force. Kesselring's rapid assembly of reinforcements and determined counter-attacks soon saw

VI Corps penned up under heavy pressure. In the defence of the beachhead 1 Recce's firepower proved an asset, as did the aggressive spirit created by Reconnaissance Corps training. After fighting off a major enemy counter-attack in early February, 1 Recce found itself on the front pages of the British press; *The Times* dubbed them the 'thin red line', and commented that 'Their spirited interpretation of their defensive role proved a decisive factor in countering the enemy's first testing thrust against the beachhead'. Nevertheless, these German assaults drove the infantry out of the positions known as 'The Thumb' and 'The Factory'.

Throughout February the regiment patrolled, fought off counter-attacks, and tried to dodge shelling and air raids, before being deployed as infantry to fill gaps in 1st Div's order of battle, by now reduced to about 50 per cent strength. Their CO, LtCol Paddy Brett, thought that serving as infantry would cause 'rustiness'; but this fear proved groundless during the Anzio break-out of 23 May, when a battlegroup (Brettforce) was formed under his command to lead the way in 1st Div's sector, between the Carroceto road and 5th Div on the extreme west flank. By early June the Germans were falling back towards and through Rome, and 1 Recce was able to rest for the first time in months.

LtCol Frederick Cotton (right) of 46 Recce died from head wounds received in the early stages of Operation 'Olive' in the last week of August 1944. Here he wears the khaki beret, and the Recce Corps lanyard in green-and-yellow twist (on the left shoulder for officers). The Recce arm-of-service strip is visible below the 46th Div sign – a green 'Sherwood Forest oak' outlined white, on a black square. (IWM NA 2199)

When 4 Recce were transferred to Greece in January 1945 they took their Staghounds with them. These troopers display a variety of cold-weather clothing as they pose for a shot for the album – leather and animal-skin jerkins, and cut-down raincoats and overcoats. (Author's collection, via Basil Goldman)

During March 1944, 5 Recce had also arrived at Anzio, for what their historian described as a 'nerve-racking and rather eerie experience'. When the break-out came 5 Recce was glad to return to a mobile role; during the race to the Tiber the regiment captured two companies from the Folgore Parachute Div, an Italian Fascist formation still fighting alongside the Germans.

The break-out from Anzio was planned to coincide with the smashing of the Gustav Line in the final battle of Cassino, and Reconnaissance Corps units involved on that sector included 4, 44, 46 and 56 Recce. During the pursuit phase of Operation 'Diadem' the recce regiments were in their element; but the advance ground to a standstill at Lake Trasimene, where the Germans sought to delay the Allies while they prepared their next major positions along the Gothic Line. Once again a battlegroup built around a recce regiment – Chavasseforce, including 56 Recce – led the way. Protecting the flank of 6th South African Armd Div's advance, Chavasseforce raced from Orvieto to the shores of Lake Trasimene in nine days, killing some 145 Germans, taking 121 prisoners, capturing or destroying about 30 guns and mortars, 56 machine guns, more than 30 vehicles, and six two-man tankettes; they also 'bagged' a German cinema unit. Thereafter 56 Recce was relieved by 4 Recce, and finally left Italy for rest, refitting and training in Egypt.

Before the Italian campaign stalled yet again, 4 Recce were able to work in the pure recce role for a time and, in early August 1944, fired their new 75mm self-propelled guns for the first time while supporting a successful infantry attack on the monastery at Incontro. After seven weeks of operations 4 Recce reached the River Arno, where they were relieved by 1 Recce. In mid September the regiment saw action again, during 4th Div's steady slog northwards to Forli, where 4 Recce's halftrack-mounted guns 'fired fast and often at targets in Ronco village and north-east of Forli'. By the end of 1944 this unit, now equipped with US Staghound heavy armoured cars, had been withdrawn from Italy for operations in Greece in the aftermath of German withdrawal from that country, to help prevent the attempted takeover by the Communist ELAS guerrillas.

* * *

The Eighth Army's attempt to break the eastern, Adriatic, sector of the Gothic Line – Operation 'Olive' – opened at midnight on 25/26 August 1944, with British V Corps on the left of the Canadian and Polish corps. Fighting in support of both infantry and armoured units, at various times 46 Recce performed standard recce duties, served as defensive troops, and provided carrier patrols to support Sappers in route recconnaissance, mine clearance and 'special tasks'. Six patrols, each of

From Italy, some regiments went to Palestine for a spell of reorganization and training before their next operational posting; this Humber Mk IV of 46 Recce is on an exercise. It has been neatly repainted in two-tone camouflage – possibly 'light stone' (sand) and terracotta red-brown. Visible markings are the C Sqn circle on the turret, a circled yellow '9' bridging code on the near side of the glacis, the 46th Div oaktree in green on a white square on the nearside mudguard, and opposite it the divisional recce regiments' usual green-over-blue square with the white '41' tactical serial. (IWM E 28649)

two carriers with a No.19 set and a despatch rider, were assigned to Sapper support. At the same time a new principle of patrolling was established: if a recce patrol reported an objective clear, it was to stay in position until the rest of the troop arrived to consolidate. Traffic control duties were added to 46 Recce's list of responsibilities in November; later in the month its remit was broadened even further when the SP Bty and Mortar Tp joined the medium machine guns of 9th Manchesters (46th Div's MG battalion) in a harassing fire programme supporting a 139 Inf Bde attack. By early December, 46 Recce was at Forli, still performing a miscellany of duties; and in January 1945, 46th Div joined 4th Div in Greece.

* * *

By August 1944, 1 Recce had reorganized its assault troops, which were now equipped with US M3 half-tracks supported by eight 75mm SPGs; these latter would 'fill a long felt want of immediate fire support during recce tasks'. In mid August the regiment moved close to Florence before mounting patrols in support of Operation 'Olive'; but as the impetus

Photographed in Palestine in January 1945, this Humber Mk IV crew from 1 Recce have smartened up for an inspection. They wear the black RAC beret with Recce badge and – unusually on KD shirtsleeve order – they all display 'Reconnaissance' shoulder titles. Two sport shoulder strap slides bearing the white triangle of 1st Div over the Recce arm-of-service strip, and also the ribbon of the First Army Africa Star; and two the Recce lanyard, on the right shoulder for other ranks. (IWM E 31286)

of that operation faded, 1 Recce created a special force – a second Brettforce – with artillerymen and engineers acting as infantry, 'to hold [the] Rignano feature in event of Monte Grande being overrun'. The regiment saw out the end of 1944 in the infantry role, enduring regular shelling, mortaring and machine-gun fire.

Such was also the lot of 44 Recce, which had returned to Italy in July 1944, and 56 Recce, which had returned in September. The latter had replaced their Humber armoured cars with American M8 Greyhounds, but were then deployed as infantry. In the final six months of the war in Italy the infantry role dominated the routine of the recce regiments still serving there – 1, 44 and 56 Recce; 5 Recce had also departed, and was to see action again in the closing phase of operations in North-West Europe.

As US Fifth and British Eighth Armies gathered their strength for the final assault in Italy, both 44 and 56 Recce held positions along the Senio river facing an enemy who was, at times, only yards away. Conditions were akin to those of the Great War, with trench raids, tunnelling and close-range mortaring. Neither regiment was sorry to leave such duty to take part in Eighth Army's Operation 'Buckland', but the speed of advance was such that 44 Recce was assigned to support duties and only entered combat quite late in the fighting. To their chagrin, in the race to be the first Allied troops into Venice the regiment were pipped to the post by a battalion of the Queen's Royal Regiment.

Their counterparts in 56 Recce played an important part in the advance through the Argenta Gap, and saw much action as they patrolled vigorously and reconnoitred for several formations. After

An M8 Greyhound armoured car of 6 Tp, 56 Recce was the first Eighth Army vehicle to cross into Austria from Italy, by the Plöcken Pass at 10.00am on 7 May 1945. America's most used armoured car of the war, the Greyhound was fast – 56mph – and had a range of 350 miles; however, with a combat weight of nearly 9 tons, its cross-country performance was not as good as the six-wheel layout might suggest. It was armed with a 37mm main gun and a co-axial .30cal MG. (Author's collection, via 56 Recce OCA)

three weeks of mobile fighting the regiment disengaged, having lost just seven dead and 17 wounded during this phase – light casualties, for the considerable action it had seen. Following the German surrender in May 1945 units of Eighth Army moved into Austria; and it was a Greyhound crew from 56 Recce who had the distinction of being the first soldiers of that army across the border.

* * *

For those regiments sent to Greece there was a short period of activity, but the worst of the civil war was over by the time 4 and 46 Recce arrived; ELAS was already being chased into the mountains, and although patrols were carried out neither regiment saw any significant action. Although 46 Recce returned to Italy it was too late to see further active service there, while 4 Recce remained in Greece until it was disbanded.

See Plate E1: this photo shows the front markings of Lt Allen's Humber Mk IV armoured car 'Davenport' of 161 Recce. The car is shrouded in very light, gauzy camouflage netting tied to a branch in the hedge line; and note the very high vantage point of the commander when seated on top of the turret. Just visible to the right of the driver's port is a mid-colour vertical bar and white '3', presumably identifying squadron and troop. (Northern Whig)

NORTH-WEST EUROPE

Of the seaborne assault divisions on D-Day, two deployed elements of their recce regiments: 3rd and 50th Divs, with 3 and 61 Recce respectively. It was not expected that either could perform a normal reconnaissance role in the initial stages, but both were to provide contact detachments and communications on the beaches, as well as assisting with traffic control. Although 61 Recce had been planned to lead a small force from 8 Armd Bde towards Villers Bocage on D-Day, this was cancelled due to problems in landing all the necessary troops.

On the evening of D-Day, 6th Abn Armd Recce Regt arrived by glider at Ranville and was soon deploying, including its two heavy

The same Northern Ireland District three-bar-gate sign, and the same squadron bar and 3 Troop sign, are displayed on the rear of this Humber LRC; a smoke bomb has just burst ahead of it in a narrow Ulster lane. (Tank Museum 2077/C3)

troops, each with four Tetrarch light tanks flown across the Channel in Hamilcar gliders.

A week later 49th (West Riding) Div landed, bringing with it 49 Recce; at the end of the month 15 (Scottish) Recce disembarked at Arromanches, followed quickly by 53 (Welsh) Recce. Also ashore at the end of June, but left out of battle, was 43 (Wessex) Recce, which had suffered the loss of 180 dead and another 150 injured when an acoustic mine exploded under the troopship *Derry Cunihy* on 24 June. The regiment's casualties were replaced by a squadron from 161 (Green Howards) Recce, which became the new A Sqn, and retained Green Howards cap badges. Finally, 59 Recce landed with 59th (Staffordshire) Div at the end of July. The 51st (Highland) Div landed in Normandy from the evening of D-Day, with 2nd Derbyshire Yeomanry in the reconnaissance role; the regiment did not wear the Corps badge, but did use the identity serial '41' on its vehicles, and is regarded as an honorary unit of the Corps – their CO, LtCol Pearce Serocold, had been the chief instructor at the Reconnaissance Training Centre.

For all the regiments that served throughout the battles for Normandy the experience was similar. There was little chance for true recce work on this enclosed battlefield, but what few opportunities existed were seized and, as elsewhere, the regiments carried out many other tasks asked of them by their parent formations. Units held the line as infantry, made sweeps with carriers and assault troops, provided flank protection for attacking formations, and used their AT guns to good

As the landing of a liberation army in North-West Europe drew closer, recce regiments in Britain were re-equipping with a variety of AFVs. The Daimler armoured car, with a 2pdr main gun, proved highly successful – and this photo reminds us that what looks right usually performs well. The Daimler had a combat weight of just under 7½ tons, a top speed of 50mph and a range of 205 miles; it was highly nimble, and popular with its crews. (Tank Museum 2803/F6)

Also from the Daimler stable was the Dingo scout car, used in large numbers by 52 (Lowland) Recce and, to a much lesser extent, by other units. Capable of 55mph, it had a range of 200 miles and a two-man crew. This vehicle does not yet carry unit markings. (IWM STT 8201)

effect, as well as discharging the more mundane tasks of traffic control and contact detachments. With each operation launched to wear down the German forces at the eastern end of the beachhead, recce units went into action alongside the heavy armour, and took similarly heavy casualties during a campaign of attrition as harsh as the Western Front of 1915–18.

A few episodes will have to stand for the whole. When Caen finally fell to British forces on 9 July, after a month of fighting, the first troops to enter the devastated ruins were detachments of 3 Recce. In the shadow of Mont Pincon, Lt Truman's carrier troop from B Sqn, 61 Recce carried out a spectacular operation to clear an enemy strongpoint, their success prompting a burst of spontaneous applause from watching British infantrymen. As 43 Recce carried out one of its first true reconnaissance tasks in France, B Sqn was delayed by the presence of German tanks on the road it was to take. A rocket attack by RAF Typhoons failed to shift the Panzers, but these finally withdrew when infantry from 43rd Div captured nearby high ground; when B Sqn moved forward again, it too was attacked by Typhoons – fortunately, the rockets missed the squadron's half-tracks.

As Allied forces closed in on the Falaise Pocket, 59 Recce provided patrols and right-flank protection for 59th Div, but the recce troops were critical of the infantry battalions with whom they were working: 'It would appear that the infantry are not aware of the role of [a] reconnaissance regiment', noted the war diary. It was believed that this was due to the absorption of many replacements for battle casualties, since co-operation and understanding had been much better in training. However, there were to be no opportunities to improve the situation; British casualties had been so high that Gen Montgomery decided to disband formations to provide reinforcements for others. The first to go was 59th (Stafforshire) Div, the most junior in British Second Army, and on 21 August the men of 59 Recce were told that their regiment was to be disbanded and its soldiers posted as reinforcements for other Reconnaissance Corps units.

* * *

With the Germans finally driven from Normandy in the last week of August, 6 Abn Armd Recce, which had replaced its little Tetrarchs with Cromwell tanks, was at last withdrawn to England; the regiment had been in action from D-Day to 26 August with almost no respite. Now the other recce units were able to demonstrate their speed during the pursuit to the Seine; the first British troops to reach that river were 43 Recce, who led the advance of XXX Corps. Also racing ahead were 15 (Scottish) Recce, with Royal Engineers armoured vehicles in support. The Welshmen of 53 Recce also crossed the Seine on 30 August; this regiment had written its own little piece of history when a troop from A Sqn became the first British soldiers to link up with the Americans

Humber also produced a scout car that was used by Recce units. Heavier and larger than the Dingo, it nevertheless had a slightly higher top road speed of 60mph, and the same range of about 200 miles. (Tank Museum 2085/D4)

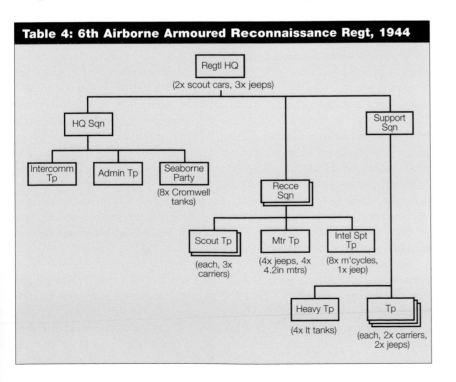

Table 4: 6th Airborne Armoured Reconnaissance Regt, 1944

- Regtl HQ (2x scout cars, 3x jeeps)
  - HQ Sqn
    - Intercomm Tp
    - Admin Tp
    - Seaborne Party (8x Cromwell tanks)
  - Recce Sqn
    - Scout Tp (each, 3x carriers)
    - Mtr Tp (4x jeeps, 4x 4.2in mtrs)
    - Intel Spt Tp (8x m'cycles, 1x jeep)
      - Heavy Tp (4x lt tanks)
      - Tp (each, 2x carriers, 2x jeeps)
  - Support Sqn

For the Normandy invasion 6th Abn Armd Recce deployed two heavy troops each of four Tetrarch light tanks, flown across in giant Hamilcar gliders; several crashed on landing at Ranville on the evening of D-Day. The Tetrarch mounted the same 2pdr gun turret as the Daimler armoured car; although hopelessly outclassed by battle tanks and SP guns, it did offer some immediate armoured support to Airborne troops fighting with only light scales of weapons during the critical first phase of a landing. (IWM KID 1534)

near Trun after the closing of the Falaise Pocket. This followed an eventful spell during which A Sqn had been 'shelled by the Yanks, Canadians and British, not to mention Jerry', but had also taken more than 2,000 prisoners, and liberated some of their own men who had been captured earlier.

Once across the Seine the Allied armies moved rapidly across France in what became known as the 'great swan', and the recce regiments were in their element. 53 (Welsh) Recce, under command of 7th Armd Div, raced for the Somme and then the Low Countries. On 1 September the Welsh troopers covered no less than 55 miles, through villages that went mad with joy. At one point a patrol under Sgt Robbie Robinson came across an elderly Frenchman sitting in an armchair in the middle of the road, sucking on a clay pipe. Under the chair a mound of horse manure covered a Teller mine; the old man had been sitting over it for three hours, to make sure no British soldier ran over it. The patrol removed and disarmed the mine, before filling a steel helmet with cigarettes and tobacco to thank the 'brave old boy', who had probably saved several soldiers' lives. On 7 September, 53 Recce entered Belgium.

61 Recce had also crossed the border, taking on its way about 4,000 prisoners and fighting several brisk actions. In one such incident, at the Gheel bridgehead, C Sqn's armoured cars went to the aid of beleaguered infantry who had endured several counter-attacks. The armoured cars 'fought their way forward like tanks throughout the day, shooting off all their ammunition. The whole squadron did a great day's work, but the casualties were heavy.'

It was mid September before 3 Recce crossed into Belgium, after a short rest to recover from their travails in Normandy. Re-equipped with Daimler armoured cars, the regiment provided a traffic-control group for 3rd Div's assault crossing of the Escaut Canal; during this operation Capt Brough made frequent crossings in a rubber boat, braving the fire of a German 20mm flak cannon. By the end of the month 3 Recce were in the Netherlands, and wondering 'what sort of an enemy General Winter would be in this part of Europe'.

Operation 'Market-Garden'
Montgomery's uncharacteristically bold plan to use the Allied airborne reserve to gain a decisive victory before the end of 1944 is too well known to need detailed repetition here. Two American and one British airborne divisions were to seize bridges across the rivers Maas, Waal and Neder Rijn at Grave, Nijmegen and Arnhem respectively (Operation 'Market'). These bridges were to be held while British XXX Corps advanced along a land corridor to Arnhem and thence into Germany itself, thereby outflanking the northern limits of the Siegfried Line (Operation 'Garden'). The furthest bridge, at Arnhem, was assigned to British 1st Abn Div; with the bridge taken, 52nd (Lowland) Div – now an air-portable formation – was to be flown into nearby Deelen airfield. Thus two recce units that had so far seen no service in NW Europe would be committed to battle: 1st Abn Recce Squadron and 52 (Lowland) Recce Regiment.

In the familiar story of Arnhem the role of 1st Abn Recce Sqn is less well known. Under command of Maj Freddie Gough, the squadron, equipped with jeeps armed with Vickers K-guns, was to carry out a *coup de main* strike to seize Arnhem bridge and hold it until the division's main body arrived. Gough considered this a misuse of his squadron, and believed that his three troops ought to precede each element of the division as they advanced from the DZs/LZs towards Arnhem, in true

LtCol W.P.Serocold, CO of 2nd Derbyshire Yeomanry, the reconnaissance regiment for 51st (Highland) Div in NW Europe. Previously, Pearce Serocold had been second-in-command of 61 Recce, and then Chief Instructor at the Recce Training Centre. (Author's collection)

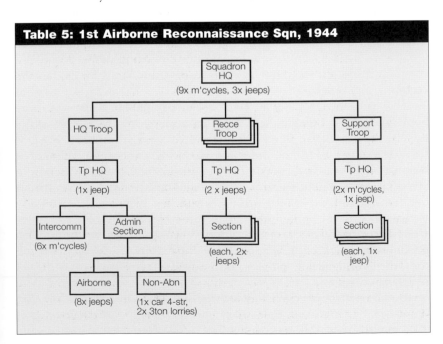

Table 5: 1st Airborne Reconnaissance Sqn, 1944

- Squadron HQ (9x m'cycles, 3x jeeps)
  - HQ Troop
    - Tp HQ (1x jeep)
      - Intercomm (6x m'cycles)
      - Admin Section
        - Airborne (8x jeeps)
        - Non-Abn (1x car 4-str, 2x 3ton lorries)
  - Recce Troop
    - Tp HQ (2 x jeeps)
      - Section (each, 2x jeeps)
  - Support Troop
    - Tp HQ (2x m'cycles, 1x jeep)
      - Section (each, 1x jeep)

Daimler Mk I armoured car of A Sqn, 2nd Derbyshire Yeomanry supporting Highland infantry during the advance into the Low Countries, autumn 1944; for marking details, see Plate E2. (IWM B 11222)

Recce fashion: in this way the best approach might be identified. However, Gough was obliged to conform to the flawed divisional plan, and to deploy the squadron as a light strike force. To overcome the tactical drawbacks that he anticipated, Gough asked for twin Vickers mountings for his jeeps, and for three Hamilcar gliders to carry a reinforcing troop of Tetrarch light tanks of 6 Abn Armd Recce; neither request was granted.

Gliders carried the squadron's heavy equipment while the men parachuted from Dakotas, but their supporting 9 Field Co RE never linked up with them. Once assembled, the jeeps advanced towards their objective, using the standard leap-frogging tactics refined in training. However, No.8 Section drove into an ambush and its men were killed or captured. Following a number of clashes with German troops the remainder of the squadron reached the objective, to find the northern end of Arnhem bridge held by men of 2nd Para Bn and other scattered troops. Gough's men reinforced Maj Frost's perimeter; but communications were in disarray due to faulty radios, and the divisional commander, MajGen Urquhart, was unaware that the recce men had reached the bridge.

The presence of two mauled Panzer divisions resting in the immediate area had not been taken into account by the planners, and the Germans were able to bring considerable firepower to bear on the

Arnhem/Oosterbeek perimeters. Instead of being relieved speedily, the lightly equipped and supplied Airborne troops were besieged for the next week – and 52nd (Lowland) Div was never committed. With the failure of XXX Corps to reach Arnhem, the order was given for 1st Abn Div to withdraw across the river as best they could. Some of 1st Abn Recce Sqn managed to escape, but many – including Maj Gough – were taken prisoner.

Three other recce regiments had parts to play in 'Market-Garden': 15 (Scottish), 43 (Wessex) and 52 (Lowland). For a week 15 Recce protected a vital supply road for the troops at Nijmegen and Arnhem, before deploying as infantry. 43 Recce, with 12th Bn King's Royal Rifle Corps, provided defence against counter-attacks on XXX Corps' eastern flank; in one incident, men of 10 Tp intercepted German frogmen placing explosive charges on the bridges at Nijmegen. When 1st Abn Div was ordered to withdraw, troops of 43 Recce helped cover their retreat.

Deprived of its original planned role, 52 Recce arrived in Son, where the regiment came under command of US 101st Abn Div; in their windproof smocks and rimless RAC helmets the recce troopers had an almost German appearance in poor light, but fortunately there were no tragic incidents. Moving to the Grave area, the regiment was soon in action against an enemy counter-attack that broke through the corridor to Arnhem, and two squadrons took part in the operation to restore it. The regiment also had the doubtful distinction of being probably the first reconnaissance unit ever to come under attack from jet aircraft, when Luftwaffe Me 262s strafed and bombed its positions, causing some casualties.

Humber Mk IVs lead Universal carriers and White M3A1 scout cars of 15 (Scottish) Recce into Belgium, September 1944. Ammo boxes have been fixed to the mudguards and glacis for stowage, and the markings have been shifted down to the nose plate. The tall, boxy silhouette of the Humber armoured car looks shocking to eyes accustomed to the tank designer's long struggle to achieve a low, squat, rounded shape for the sake of stability, concealment and protection; but the recce car was never intended to cross seriously rough terrain, or to survive the fire of tanks or AT guns. It relied on its road speed, and its commander's binoculars, to stay out of trouble; and the Humber's height gave him a longer view, raising his head about ten feet above the ground. (IWM BU 823)

Men of 15 (Scottish) Recce are the centre of attention in this Belgian town; as patrols probed forwards 'they were greeted with wild enthusiasm, flowers, wine, cheers and kisses from the local populace, delighted at this evidence of liberation'. These Jocks appear to have arrived in an American White M3A1 scout car, its mudguards marked with the tactical serial – here with an unexplained white base bar – and the divisional sign. Although used to some extent by recce units, the M3A1 lacked overhead protection and was seriously underpowered. One soldier (fourth from right) still wears the khaki beret, the others black; the sergeant (centre) displays the shoulder title and divisional sign on his sleeve; the very dark BD worn by the warrant officer (right foreground) is unexplained – perhaps black-dyed denim fatigues? (IWM B 11269)

Winter in the Low Countries

In 21st Army Group, attention now turned to the left flank and the clearing of the Scheldt estuary, vital to allow the port of Antwerp to be used to shorten the Allies' long logistical 'tail'. For this task I Corps included 49th (West Riding) and 52nd (Lowland) Divisions. It was difficult terrain in which to fight, as 52 Recce discovered on the Leopold Canal line: 'At first we held the position with two squadrons, but the ground was deeply flooded, only the raised roadways, so common in Holland, being above water and they were always heavily mined and covered by intense fire from the enemy'. Relieved of this task, 52 Recce returned to its division, which was taking part in the amphibious operation to clear North and South Beveland and Walcheren; 52 Recce was to cut the German escape route across North Beveland and Schouwen. The regiment was highly successful, rounding up many prisoners and thwarting a German raiding party.

At the beginning of October 1944, 49 Recce was leading its division's advance on Turnhout; at one stage C Sqn beat off a counter-attack by German paratroopers, inflicting heavy casualties. Then followed a spell holding the line before the unit joined Clarkeforce – an armoured group that included 107th Regt RAC – in an advance from Ryckevorsel to Kruisland north of Antwerp. The squadrons had 'to fight their way forward against stubborn opposition from enemy infantry, paratroops and self-propelled guns… most of the work had to be done on foot because of the extreme difficulty and open nature of the country; nevertheless progress was quite rapid and upwards of 150 prisoners of

(continued on page 41)

UNITED KINGDOM, 1941–42
1: Second lieutenant, 1941
2: Corporal, 48 Recce, 1941
3: RSM Harrison, RTC Lockerbie, 1942

A

NORTH AFRICA & ITALY, 1942–44
1: Trooper, 51 (Highland) Recce; Egypt, Oct 1942
2: Trooper, 46 Recce; Sangro river, Italy, Oct 1943
3: LtCol K.G.F.Chavasse, DSO*, 56 Recce; Italy, summer 1944

B

NORTH-WEST EUROPE, 1944–45
1: Armoured car commander; Low Countries, winter 1944
2: Sergeant Millroy, DCM, 15 (Scottish) Recce, Dec 1944
3: Trooper, Assault Troop, 3 Recce; France, summer 1944
4: Lieutenant, 52 (Lowland) Recce, 1944–45

C

VEHICLES

1: Humber Mk III LRC, HQ 56 Recce; Sicily, Aug 1943

2: Humber Mk IV armoured car, 2 Tp, A Sqn, 53 (Welsh) Recce;
Rhineland, Feb 1945

D

VEHICLES
1: Humber Mk IV; 3 Tp, D Sqn, 161 (Green Howards) Recce; Northern Ireland, April 1944
2: Daimler Mk I, A Sqn, 2nd Derbyshire Yeomanry, 51st (Highland) Div; Low Countries, autumn 1944

E

AIRBORNE RECCE
1: Jeep, A Tp, 1st Abn Recce Sqn; Arnhem, Sept 1944
2: Sgt, 6th Abn Armd Recce; UK, spring 1944
3: Maj C.F.H.Gough, 1st Abn Recce Sqn;
  Arnhem, Sept 1944

F

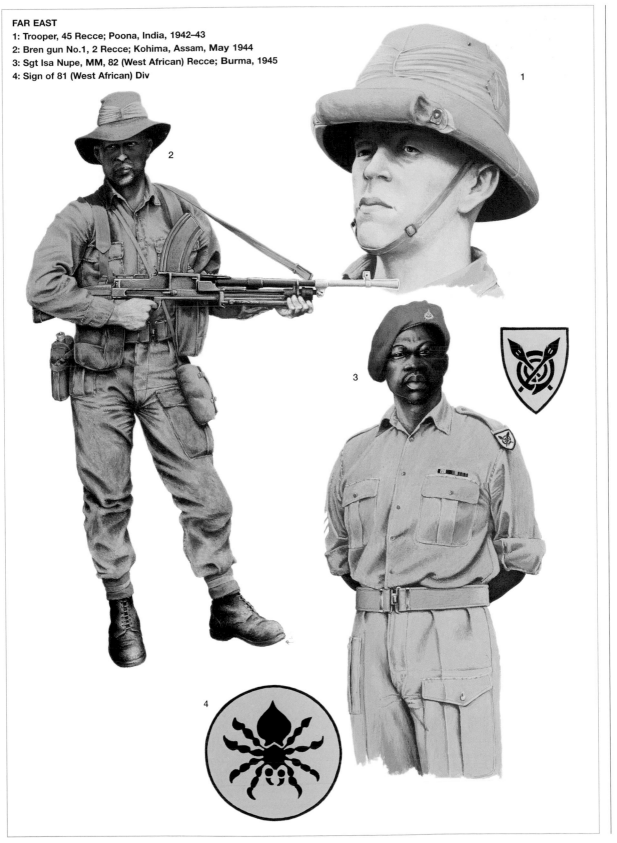

FAR EAST

1: Trooper, 45 Recce; Poona, India, 1942–43
2: Bren gun No.1, 2 Recce; Kohima, Assam, May 1944
3: Sgt Isa Nupe, MM, 82 (West African) Recce; Burma, 1945
4: Sign of 81 (West African) Div

G

To add to the misery of heavy rainfall in the very cold, wet winter of 1944/45, the Germans flooded large areas of the Low Countries. The going is difficult for this Humber scout car and Universal carrier of 43 (Wessex) Recce; and note the car commander wearing the 'pixie suit'. (Author's collection)

war were taken during the operation.' A major infantry assault was needed to crack German defences on the Mark Canal, and 49 Recce provided a 'Phantom' wireless net to cover this battle. By the end of November the regiment had also taken part in Operation 'Chester', a XII Corps attack to clear the east bank of the Maas and capture Blerick, near Venlo on the Dutch-German border; once again, much of the work had to be done on foot.

The final winter of the war in Europe was one of bitter weather and even more bitter fighting, as the enemy strove to keep the Western Allies off German soil. By the end of November 1944 most of the recce regiments in NW Europe were in the Low Countries, although 61 Recce had been told of its impending disbandment, since its parent 50th Div was to be broken up. Its CO, LtCol Philip Brownrigg, obtained a stay of execution by appealing to XXX Corps' commander, LtGen Brian Horrocks. By Christmas the regiment was again facing disbandment, but was again saved, this time by the German Ardennes offensive. This saw it committed, with 11th Armd Div, to the line of the Maas from Namur to Givet, 'and then gradually patrolling farther forward, until towards the end of the campaign we had a battleground of our own with a front of twenty miles between the Americans and the rest of the British'. When hard frost, mines and demolished bridges made vehicle movement almost impossible, one enterprising officer of 61 Recce took to horseback to reconnoitre in the American sector – a feat reported by the BBC. The axe of disbandment finally fell on 61 Recce in January 1945; during its brief life the regiment had earned a DSO, 11 MCs, a DCM, five MMs, three Croix de Guerre and three MBEs.

The historian of 3 Recce described that regiment's vigil along the Maas, from October 1944 to February 1945, as 'hard and often dangerous work'. There were OPs to be manned, while the regiment also provided personnel for a mobile force which included 2nd Household Cavalry Regt and two squadrons of the Inns of Court Regt, to protect the left flank of an offensive against Overloon and Venray. Tasked to hold the river line to Vierlingsbeek, 3 Recce captured that

A Humber Mk IV of A Sqn, 53 (Welsh) Recce, named 'Laughing Boy III', engages enemy positions near Goch in Germany, February 1945. The car commander, Lt James Ferguson, was asked by the official photographer to sit a little more out of the turret 'to make a better photograph', but felt justified in declining, since German MG42s were returning fire. For marking details, see Plate D2. (IWM B 14830)

village in a tough action, and held it against frequent German raids. A similar experience befell 15 (Scottish) Recce, which had taken part in the liberation of Tilburg at the end of October, before deploying with its division to strengthen US 7th Armd Div following a German counter-attack near Helmond.

Observation and listening posts were also the lot of 43 Recce, which was responsible for some 200 Dutch resistance fighters and took under command a battery of SPGs from the Essex Yeomanry. For the first and only time the regiment's new 6-pdr AT guns were used in anger – harassing enemy boats on the Waal. On 18 December, A and C Sqns became the first Reconnaissance Corps elements to enter Germany itself, as part of XXX Corps' thrust on Geilenkirchen. However, appalling weather made the roads and fields almost impassable, and German counter-attacks stopped further forward movement. When 52 Recce relieved 43 Recce on 18 December, the Wessex troopers looked forward to a rest; but the Germans launched their Ardennes offensive that night, and 43 Recce was diverted to help hold the line of the Maas and form a counter-attack force.

During October 1944, 53 Recce had served in the 'Island' close to Arnhem, and came under command of US 101st Abn Div before taking part in XII Corps' Operation 'Alan', an attack through s'Hertogenbosch, Tilburg and Breda to clear the Scheldt. In this offensive the regiment was joined by 340 SP Bty and 1st East Lancs Regt in Kangaroos – armoured personnel carriers improvised from de-gunned Priest SPGs. Tilburg, Breda and Roosendaal were taken and the enemy threat to Antwerp was blunted. In early December, 53 Recce took part in Operation 'Windup', an artillery programme 'to cause the enemy the maximum casualties and discomfort in his positions on the east bank of the Maas by bringing at irregular intervals concentrated fire from all guns in the Division'. This fireplan involved 53 Recce's AT guns, 'to the great delight of their gunners'; the regiment's mortars were also used. Relieved by the Inns of Court Regt on 18 December, 53 Recce were soon back in the line during the Ardennes scare; they deployed along the Maas from Dinant to Namur under command of 6th Abn Div, alongside 6 Armd Recce Regiment. Neither unit was given a significant role in XXX Corps' offensive in early January, and following a spell on defensive duties 6th Armd Abn Recce returned to Britain at the end of the month.

Advance to the Rhine

With the Ardennes threat defeated, Montgomery intended to take 21st Army Group through the Reichswald forest and up to the Rhine in two operations, 'Grenade' and 'Veritable'. To prepare the way for these, Operation 'Blackcock', to clear the 'Roer triangle', was assigned to 7th Armd and 52nd (Lowland) Divs with assistance from 43rd (Wessex) Div and 8th Armoured Brigade. To free up infantry, 43 Recce held part of the line, while 52 Recce advanced in a blinding snowstorm on frozen roads that made movement very difficult, especially for the AT Tp's carriers. The Germans fell back gradually, 'but never without a struggle', and counter-attacks were common. B Squadron and RHQ spent 'forty-eight of the coldest hours of the whole campaign' in slit trenches at Aan Popelaar, while C Sqn at Popinus bridge had to deal with a flood of refugees as well as the enemy.

Once the Roer triangle had been cleared 52 Recce was given the unenviable task of relieving 3 Recce guarding the river line against counter-attack, which entailed a 24-hour watch in freezing conditions

A carrier of an unidentified recce unit passes two Canadian Staghounds of 12th Manitoba Dragoons (18th Armd Car Regt) near Doetinchem in the Netherlands. (National Archives of Canada: PA 131693; Michael M.Dean)

under occasional shell and mortar fire. All this time 3 Recce, with two companies of Dutch resistance fighters under command, had been based along the Maas in the villages of Groeningen, Vortum and Sambeek; on one night 22 degrees of frost were recorded. The regiment and its Dutch comrades carried out interdiction against enemy patrols, as well as harassing the Germans along the far bank with their MMGs, .50in Browning MGs and the firepower of their gunner support units. Not content with this activity, 3 Recce also took the battle to the enemy with Wilforce – two carrier troops from A Sqn under Maj Wilson, that patrolled the enemy side of the Maas from about 10 January. True to the Corps' tradition of versatility, Wilforce became skilled in the handling of assault boats, and also 'achieved proficiency in fighting in buildings and night patrolling, even taking advantage of bright moonlight on the snow'.

The Yorkshiremen of 49 Recce had similar experiences along the Waal. German retaliation to their mortar 'stonks' was sharp (although the fact that two V1 flying bombs landed near 49 Recce positions was probably coincidental). Operation 'Jock' on 21 February saw 32 recce men, Sappers and Royal Navy personnel crossing the river in LCAs and inflicting 'considerable damage on the enemy', who included Dutch soldiers of the Waffen-SS. The regiment remained on these tasks until 5 April, and became ever more adventurous in its attacks.

Four recce regiments took part in Operation 'Veritable', which began on 8 February 1945; 15 (Scottish) and 53 (Welsh) Recce were the first into action. Two squadrons of 15 Recce exploited the gap in the Siegfried Line made by their division, and reconnoitred for the advance of two mobile columns, as well as for 2nd Household Cavalry. Although the advance was stalled for two days by flooding, 15th (Scottish) Div was soon fighting its way forward, with all three squadrons of 15 Recce now in action. With its objectives achieved by 23 February, the division was withdrawn to prepare for the Rhine crossing.

Traffic control duties had been the main function of 53 Recce early in 'Veritable', but the squadrons then deployed for flank protection and fighting patrols or as infantry. With leeks in their helmets, C Sqn, with a squadron of Sherwood Rangers, formed Robinforce on St David's Day, 1 March, to protect 158 Inf Bde's left flank during the advance on Weeze. In spite of stiff resistance the squadron penetrated to a depth of one and a half miles.

As the advance continued, A Sqn covered 8 Armd Bde's right flank. 'Moving in red, troops cleared neighbouring woods with foot and mobile patrols and flushed out scattered groups of enemy soldiers, most of whom were keen to surrender'. Contact was made with British 3rd and US 35th Divs, and the regiment continued to be involved heavily until relieved by 52 (Lowland) Recce on 7 March 1945.

Probing ahead of 43rd (Wessex) Div, the troopers of 43 Recce met considerable opposition; several men were captured, but later liberated by 53 Recce. At one point the CO took a war correspondent along the Cleve–Calcar road in his LRC, only to be caught in a heavy concentration of German artillery fire as they passed through the forward infantry positions, giving the correspondent plenty of colourful copy to file. On another occasion L/Cpl Lane, a medical orderly, earned the Military Medal when he dismounted from a carrier to pick up

a wounded soldier in full view of the enemy. After the fall of Goch, 43 Recce reconnoitred the main road to Udem as well as a parallel route, meeting stiff resistance on both. After a brief pause 43 Recce were back in action within days, and remained so until 12 March, installing OPs on the Rhine. The German bridgehead west of the river – the Schlieffen position – had been eliminated, and 21st Army Group was preparing to cross the Rhine.

During XXX Corps' advance on Goch, 52nd (Lowland) Div had been on its right flank, pushing down the eastern bank of the Maas, and 52 Recce was heavily engaged. This regiment was only now reorganized 'as a normal reconnaissance regiment'; having earlier given up its tank squadron, 52 Recce had been understrength by one troop in each squadron. It had also relied on Dingo scout cars – as a result of its originally envisaged mountain role it had no heavy armoured cars. Now, however, three complete troops of reinforcements were received from the disbanded 61 Recce, and heavy armoured cars also arrived. On 8 February the regiment relieved 3 Recce at Boxmeer, where it became the core of a strong battlegroup that included 8 Canadian Recce, two platoons (MMGs and 4.2in mortars) from 7th Manchesters, and 1st Mountain Regiment, Royal Artillery.

Following some patrolling across the Maas using assault boats, 52 Recce moved to Gennep from where, on 16 February, C Sqn struck out on the difficult road to Afferden. With the advance on the left stalled before Goch, the regiment deployed along the obstacle, where it remained until the end of the month, suffering heavy shelling and

Dingo and MMG carrier of 6th Abn Armd Recce in Schwerin, Germany, April 1945. Note the clutter of stowage on the vehicles, and the mix of 'pixie suits' and BD worn by the soldiers. This regiment had been formed in January 1944 from 6th Abn Div's light tank squadron; the latter had been an RAC unit but, on expansion to regimental status, it was considered appropriate that it should bear the Reconnaissance Corps badge, although many personnel continued wearing their original unit insignia on their maroon berets. Although three badges are visible here, none of them is that of the Recce Corps. (John Banbery)

Fraternization: a Red Army soldier inspects a Dingo and a US-supplied scout car or half-track of 6th Abn Armd Recce at Wismar, May 1945. (John Banbery)

mortaring; at one point a counter-mortar officer in the area declared that there were more German mortar positions in that sector than Intelligence had believed were held by the entire German army in the West. On 1 March the regiment took part in a fresh assault, supported by 6th Highland Light Infantry, a troop of Churchill tanks from 34 Tank Bde, a mountain battery and a section of MMGs; the assault was successful, and earned the regiment's first Military Cross for Maj James Stormonth-Darling. Thereafter 52 Recce was relieved by 45 Commando, and moved to Geldern to relieve 53 Recce. Another week of action followed before the regiment was pulled out of the line to prepare for the Rhine crossing.

Across the Rhine

The crossing – Operation 'Plunder' – began on the night of 23/24 March 1945. British XII and XXX Corps assaulted over a 12-mile front between Rees and Wesel; also involved was the US XVIII Abn Corps, with British 6th Abn Div under command. Of the Reconnaissance Corps regiments in NW Europe the only unit not involved was 49 (West Riding) Recce. As well as 15, 52 and 53 Recce in XII Corps, and 3 and 43 Recce in XXX Corps, 6 Abn Armed Recce was also deployed in the US airborne corps, while 2nd Derbyshire Yeomanry reconnoitred for 51st (Highland) Div in XXX Corps.

The first assault troops crossed the Rhine in Buffalo LVTs under cover of darkness on the night of 23 March. Although the Germans resisted fiercely their defence lacked cohesion, and the attackers had achieved most of their objectives by dawn. As follow-up units crossed, the Airborne soldiers began dropping at 10.00am in Operation 'Varsity', and by dusk the first link-up with 6th Abn Div had been achieved by the leading troops of 15 (Scottish) Recce. That unit had recently traded in their Humber armoured cars for Daimlers, which had required a hasty retraining programme, but 15 Recce was ready for its part in 'Plunder'; C Sqn crossed in Buffaloes unmolested by enemy artillery, thanks to the airborne drops. By dusk the squadron had probed to Hamminkeln and had sent a patrol to the autobahn north of that town. The rest of the regiment crossed the Rhine by pontoon bridge on the morning of 26 March; by that time C Sqn was patrolling the front and filling gaps in the line, and both A and B Sqns were soon engaged on similar tasks.

After heavy fighting along the front on 27 March, 15 Recce took over the divisional left flank the next day to allow 227 Inf Bde to attack Haldern on the 29th. However, patrols from 15 Recce spotted British troops approaching Haldern from the west, which led to the cancellation of 227 Bde's operation – patrols from 3rd Div had found Haldern abandoned. Similar stories were repeated along the front; the Germans had withdrawn during the night, and a pursuit was soon under way.

In the airborne phase of the Rhine crossings, the complete force was on the ground in little more than an hour, with the light tanks (now US M22 Locusts) of 6 Abn Armd Recce deploying into action and the regiment's mortars firing under command of the divisional CRA. By the 27th the complete regiment was taking part in the crossing of the Issel, in which three tanks were knocked out. Next day contact was made with US 17th Abn Div; patrols later pushed forward with armoured cars of the Inns of Court Regiment. Contact was made with 3 Recce on 31 March and, the next day, the regiment was driving for Greven.

On the XXX Corps front, 3 Recce had crossed on 26 March with 43 Recce following two days later. They cleared a route for 6 Guards Armd Bde and US 513th PIR as they advanced towards Munster, and also provided flank protection for a Coldstream battalion, as well as making contact with 6th Airborne Division. The flank protection role was very important, as both 3rd Div's flanks were exposed – they had outstripped 6th Abn Div to the north and US units to the south. The regiment had several very hectic days before Munster fell, and its soldiers were allowed 'our first night's sleep for days'.

The race to the Baltic

The Wessex Div's 43 Recce had replaced half their Humber armoured cars with Daimlers before crossing the Rhine, for operations along the roads to Mechelen and Anholt. Against stiff local resistance the regiment made good progress, and the Germans were retreating by 30 March. In the ensuing pursuit 43 Recce provided flank protection, although one squadron was to operate with the tanks of 8 Armoured Brigade. The war diary notes that 'resistance has almost ceased', and that, on 1 April, the regiment was 'to flood the country with armoured cars'. Further progress was made before 43 Recce withdrew to

Humber Mk IV of 49 (West Riding) Recce passing a road sign for Arnhem, en route to Utrecht on 7 May 1945. The divisional sign of a white polar bear is visible on the nearside mudguard. (NA of Canada: PA 128949: J.Ernest DeGuire)

reorganize on 4 April; it was then that they finally handed in their khaki Reconnaissance Corps berets for the black headgear of the Royal Armoured Corps, as one of the last recce regiments to make the change.

In 52 Recce, only A Sqn took part in the Rhine crossing – with a commando brigade – while the remainder carried out traffic control duties. Their Welsh comrades of 53 Recce, with no part in the initial crossing, were assigned to follow up between Rees and Wesel, and made an attack north-east through Bocholt, Stadtohn, Ahaus and Gronau before swinging right across the Ems river. Passing through 15th (Scottish) Div, the unit made good progress and, by the end of March, 53 Recce was making towards Gronau and Enschede; en route they had captured two bridges intact, putting the demolition parties to flight and thereby saving 53rd Div an estimated 11 hours and a difficult bridging operation. Once across the Weser, 53 Recce then led the way towards the Elbe and Bremen in what was described as 'tough slogging, and there was even some stonking reminiscent of Normandy as well'; but Bremen had fallen to other formations, and the regiment moved off on alternative tasks. The Welsh recce troopers finished the war in Hamburg.

In March 1945, 5th Div from Italy arrived to take part in the final push across north Germany; now equipped with Daimler armoured cars, 5 Recce joined VIII Corps' advance towards the Elbe on the British right flank. They went into action on 19 April, and on that first day two NCOs earned the Military Medal for gallantry under fire. After many skirmishes the regiment crossed the Elbe on the morning of 2 May, and was soon reconnoitring ahead of 13 and 17 Inf Brigades. In the absence of organized resistance 5 Recce moved to Neustadt, where the squadrons attempted to forge order out of chaos. Especially harrowing was the discovery of a hut full of Jewish prisoners, 'living skeletons, with legs and arms little thicker than hockey-sticks'. The local garrison surrendered, the area was handed over to 6th Abn Div, and 5 Recce moved to Travemunde, where the news of the German surrender reached them.

The other regiments in Germany shared similar experiences. Resistance was patchy, but it was the recce troopers who were the first to run into the occasional pockets of Nazi diehards, and nerves were tested by the thought that these final days would be a particularly cruel time to die. South of Lingen, 3 Recce had a sharp encounter in which Sgt T.Cottrell earned the Distinguished Conduct Medal – second only to the Victoria Cross. The regiment was soon on its way to Bremen, although a squadron was left for some days to watch a stretch of the Ems–Weser canal. As 3rd Div closed on Bremen the regiment was engaged in patrolling, reconnoitring routes or flank protection. In the final assault its role was confined to traffic control, and to deploying the AT Bty in a holding position on the left of the line. After some further patrolling the regiment was watching the Canadian right flank on the advance to Oldenburg. On 30 April, 3 Recce took its last two prisoners. When the ceasefire came at 0800 on 5 May, 'it came without the thrill and excitement most of us had expected'.

In the last weeks 15th (Scottish) Recce 'was continually in action for over a fortnight, leading first the 6th Airborne Division, [who were] riding on tanks of... Guards Armoured Division, and then our own Division for more than a hundred miles'. An average speed of 15mph was achieved, including 'stops to brush aside light resistance'. In one engagement with a Tiger tank, however, elements of B Sqn under Lt Arthur Buck were forced to withdraw after trying to knock out the tank with a 6-pounder; the Tiger drove over the gun, having already destroyed or damaged all the recce vehicles. With its own division, 15 Recce drove for Celle and then to Nettelkamp, where it had a fierce encounter with a German battlegroup; 13 vehicles were lost, five men were killed and many captured, although their captivity was brief. On 17 April, 15 Recce met 2nd SAS Regt, and the two units worked together as Frankforce. When 15 Recce crossed the Elbe, they shared their formation's distinction of being the only division of Second Army to assault the Seine, Rhine and Elbe, thus acquiring the soubriquet of 'crossing-sweepers'. On 30 April came news of Hitler's death; and on 2 May, at Hamburg, Sgt 'Tiny' Kirman of A Sqn became the 'first link in the chain of negotiations which resulted in the surrender of Hamburg and, ultimately, of the German armies in North-West Europe'.

In its last phase of operations 43 Recce was equally busy, moving towards Bremerhaven, where it ended the war. The regiment's Maj Bindon Blood and Sgt George Drake had earned an MC and a DCM respectively almost as soon as it returned to action on 8 April. During this period 43 Recce's soldiers unsurprisingly became very 'bazooka-conscious', as the terrain restricted their freedom of movement and enemy soldiers fought last-ditch actions; several men were lost to mines and shells in the last days of a war which had lasted for five and a half years.

A Humber armoured car, a Humber LRC and several jeeps of 49 Recce halt at the roadside *en route* to Utrecht. The killing is over at last – but it will probably be some time yet before any Recce trooper can drive round a blind corner without his stomach tensing up. (NA of Canada: PA 128945: J.Ernest DeGuire)

Bremen had also been an objective for 52nd (Lowland) Div, to which the city's garrison surrendered. Its 52 Recce had fought some brisk actions while searching out alternative routes to avoid demolitions, and A Sqn's cutting of the Bremen–Hamburg autobahn was one of the factors that led to the surrender. The regiment stayed in Bremen after the final German capitulation; although it was assigned to a force intended for Norway, this order was cancelled and 52 Recce remained in Germany.

The end of the war found 6th Abn Armd Recce in contact with the Red Army following a fast run to the line Lubow–Hohen–Viechlen. The regiment returned to the UK at the end of May to prepare for service against Japan, but the bombing of Hiroshima and Nagasaki saved them from that. However, a move to Palestine on internal security duties gave the regiment the distinction of being the last Recce unit to see active service.

The only regiment not to cross the Rhine into Germany was 49 Recce, which was involved in the liberation of the Netherlands and the final capture of Arnhem in mid April 1945. There followed a further advance before the regiment halted at Renswoude for negotiations for a local German surrender; C Sqn captured the bridge there, before handing it back to the Germans, to allow food convoys through for the local population and to assist in the surrender negotiations.

With the war in Europe over, the recce regiments had completed their tasks – and with distinction. Each unit except 6th Abn was engaged on a variety of occupation duties, which filled their time as men were demobilized and the regiments diminished. As disbandment drew closer, most were replaced by RAC cavalry regiments as the 'eyes' of their divisions.

THE FAR EAST

As mentioned above, the first recce unit to see action was 18 Bn, which had been shipped from Britain bound for North Africa but diverted while at sea to the Far East. After staging in India, 18 Recce followed the main body of 18th (East Anglian) Div to Singapore; they landed on 5 February 1942, in time to take part in the final battle for the island. Having lost most of their weapons and equipment when Japanese dive-bombers struck their troopship, the battalion re-equipped hastily before moving into the front line. Fighting as infantry, 18 Recce took part in several desperate actions and, as part of Thomforce, recaptured the village of Bukit Timah from the Japanese. Although by this stage surrender seemed inevitable, 18 Recce continued to hold its positions, and made counter-attacks that evicted the Japanese from some of their recent gains. With the fall of Singapore the battalion, which had suffered 55 officers and men killed in battle, marched into Japanese captivity; another 264 men would die as prisoners of war.

The memorial to 2 Recce's dead at Kohima. Below the names of those who fell is carved Binyon's exhortation: 'At the going down of the sun and in the morning, we shall remember them'. (Author's collection)

Kohima: 2 Recce

Despite the unpromising terrain over which Fourteenth Army operated in Burma, four reconnaissance regiments served in that campaign. One, 45 Recce, served in the second Chindit expedition behind Japanese lines; another, 2 Recce, played a significant role in the fighting around Kohima; and the others, 81 and 82 (West African) Recce, fought in the Arakan, where the former performed a role similar to that of the Chindits.

In early June 1942, 2 Recce arrived in Bombay. Training at Poona was interrupted by internal security duties following the arrest of Mahatma Gandhi. After a further interruption for anti-bandit duties later in the year the unit was reorganized; it added a D Sqn, while A Sqn became an Alligator squadron equipped with the US LVT-1 amphibious vehicle – a role in which it was later joined by C Squadron. These squadrons were assigned to 36th Indian Div for an operation in the Arakan region of the Burmese coast; but the plan was cancelled, the squadrons returned to the regiment, and the Alligators were given up. In March 1944, 2 Recce returned to a conventional organization with three recce squadrons, although it retained its D Sqn. It was moved to Dimapur as the Japanese Fifteenth Army

Table 6: Summary of units

Battalions/regiments served with the same-numbered infantry divisions in most cases – exceptions are noted below.

Combat units & squadron:

1st Reconnaissance Regiment
Served in Tunisia, March–May 1943; Italy, from November 1943 (including Anzio); withdrawn to Palestine, January 1945.

1st Airborne Reconnaissance Squadron
As 1st Air-Landing Reconnaissance Sqn, served briefly in Italy in autumn 1943. Virtually destroyed at Arnhem, September 1944, with rest of 1st Airborne Division.

2nd Reconnaissance Regiment
Formed from 6th Bn Loyal Regiment (North Lancs). Served in India from June 1942; Kohima campaign, April–May 1944; advanced into Burma, autumn 1944–April 1945.

2nd Derbyshire Yeomanry
Although never officially part of the Corps, this regiment enjoyed honorary status; it was assigned to **51st (Highland) Division** as its reconnaissance unit in January 1944, and served with that formation throughout the NW Europe campaign from June 1944 until May 1945. Its CO was LtCol W.P.Serocold, formerly Chief Instructor at the Recce Training Centre.

3rd Reconnaissance Regiment
Formed from 8th Bn Royal Northumberland Fusiliers. Landed in Normandy, 6 June 1944, and served throughout the NW Europe campaign until May 1945.

4th Reconnaissance Regiment
Served in Tunisia, April–May 1943; Italy, February–December 1944; withdrawn to Greece, January 1945.

5th Reconnaissance Regiment
Formed from 3rd Bn Tower Hamlets Rifles, Rifle Brigade. Served in Sicily, July–August 1943; Italy, September 1943–July 1944; withdrawn to Palestine, July 1944; in Italy, February 1945; NW Europe, March–May 1945

6th Airborne Armoured Reconnaissance Regiment
Formed from Light Tank Sqn, 6th Airborne Division; designated as reconnaissance regiment, January 1944. Landed in Normandy by glider, 6 June 1944, and served there until August; Belgium, December 1944–February 1945; Germany, March–May 1945.

15th (Scottish) Reconnaissance Regiment
Landed in Normandy late June 1944, and served throughout the NW Europe campaign until May 1945.

18th Reconnaissance Battalion
Formed from 5th Bn Loyal Regt (North Lancs). Captured in Singapore, February 1942, before cavalry nomenclature adopted by Reconnaissance Corps units.

43rd (Wessex) Reconnaissance Regiment
Formed originally as 48th Recce Bn from 5th Bn Gloucestershire Regt, and absorbed squadron from 161 (Green Howards) Recce, June/July 1944. Landed in Normandy late June 1944, and served throughout the NW Europe campaign until May 1945.

44th Reconnaissance Regiment
Served in North Africa from July 1942, as mine clearance unit for XIII Corps at El Alamein in October; when 44th (Home Counties) Division broken up for reinforcements in January 1943, regiment transferred to **56th (London) Division**. Served in Tunisia, April–May 1943; Italy, September 1943–May 1945.

45th Reconnaissance Regiment
Served in India with **70th Division** from March 1942; thereafter with **Special Force (Chindits)**, forming 45 and 54 Columns of 16 Brigade in second operation, March–May 1944; disbanded and re-formed as 2nd Bn South Staffordshire Regt, October 1944.

46th Reconnaissance Regiment
Served in Tunisia, January–May 1943. Landed at Salerno, September 1943; served in Italy until January 1945, when withdrawn to Greece.

49th (West Riding) Reconnaissance Regiment
Landed in Normandy mid June 1944, and served throughout the NW Europe campaign until May 1945.

50th Reconnaissance Battalion
Formed from 4th Bn Royal Northumberland Fusiliers, which had served in a recce role in France, 1940, with motorcycles. Served with 22 Armoured Brigade in North Africa from April 1942; destroyed in Gazala battles in late May/early June, before cavalry nomenclature was adopted.

51st (Highland) Reconnaissance Regiment
Served in North Africa from August 1942; fought as infantry at El Alamein in October; thereafter converted to lorried infantry as 14th Bn Highland Light Infantry; disbanded June 1943. From January 1944, **2nd Derbyshire Yeomanry** (see above) joined 51st (Highland) Division as reconnaissance regiment.

52nd (Lowland) Reconnaissance Regiment
Trained originally for mountain warfare, this unit included a squadron of Valentine tanks and used Daimler Dingo scout cars. Re-roled officially as an air-portable formation, in the event 52nd (Lowland) Division was shipped to NW Europe as a conventional infantry formation in October 1944, and served throughout the rest of that campaign until May 1945.

53rd (Welsh) Reconnaissance Regiment
Landed in Normandy in late June 1944, and served throughout the NW Europe campaign until May 1945.

56th Reconnaissance Regiment
The first to see action in the Reconnaissance role, this unit landed in Tunisia with **78th Division** in November 1942 and served there until May 1943; in Sicily, July–August 1943; and in Italy, September 1943–May 1945.

59th (Staffordshire) Reconnaissance Regiment
Landed in Normandy late July 1944; 59th (Staffordshire) Division broken up for reinforcements, August 1944.

61st Reconnaissance Regiment
Allocated in January 1944 to **50th (Northumbrian) Division**. Landed in Normandy on 6 June 1944, and served in the NW Europe campaign until January 1945, when the regiment was broken up for reinforcements.

81st (West African) Reconnaissance Regiment
Shipped to India in August 1943. Served in the Arakan campaigns, Burma, January–April 1944 and October 1944–January 1945.

82nd (West African) Reconnaissance Regiment
Shipped to India in July 1944. Served in the Arakan, Burma, February–May 1945.

161st (Green Howards) Reconnaissance Regiment
Formed originally as 161st Regt RAC from 12th Bn Green Howards, but transferred to Reconnaissance Corps in October 1943. Never saw action as a regiment; but one squadron, transferred into 43 Recce to replace losses in June 1944, retained Green Howards' distinctions.

GHQ Liaison Regiment ('Phantom')

Phantom operated long-range patrols driving with forward troops, or air-dropped behind enemy lines, to send information on the enemy directly to Army HQ by wireless. In early 1944 it was affiliated to the Royal Armoured Corps, after which it drew reinforcements from the Reconnaissance regiments. By the end of the war about 200 Recce men were serving with Phantom.

Other units & establishments:

38th Reconnaissance Regiment

Formed in October 1943 from 38, 47 & 55 Independent Recce Sqn; disbanded October 1944, without seeing action. In that month the regiment's title was taken over by 80 (Holding) Regt – see below.

54th Reconnaissance Regiment

Formed in July 1941 from 21st Bn Royal Fusiliers; broken up that November into 45, 54 & 76 Independent Recce Sqns. In February 1943, 45 & 54 Ind Sqns amalgamated with 15 Recce Sqn to form the new 15th (Scottish) Reconnaissance Regt; 76 Sqn became part of 80 (Holding) Regt.

80th (Holding) Regiment

Formed in January 1943 from 48, 76 & 77 Independent Recce Sqns, as a holding and training unit. Renamed 38 Recce Regt in October 1944, but continued in its holding and training role, based at Morecambe, Lancs.

Reconnaissance OCTU

At first the Corps had its own Officer Cadet Training Unit, 162 Reconnaissance OCTU, formed from the infantry battalion of the Honourable Artillery Company. In 1942, this amalgamated with 101 RAC OCTU at Sandhurst, to form 100 RAC OCTU, which remained there for the rest of the war. The Chief Instructor was LtCol N.R.Blockley, formerly CO of 5 Recce.

Reconnaissance Training Centre

Formed at Winchester in January 1941, the Centre moved to Lockerbie, Scotland, in May that year. In August 1943 it was amalgamated with 63rd Recce Training Centre, and moved to Catterick for the rest of the war.

Reconnaissance Corps Band

Authorized in January 1943, this was formed by WO I Bandmaster Charles Adams (formerly of 1st Bn Royal Scots), and was ready to perform in public by that June. As well as touring the UK, it also toured the Low Countries in 1944–45, where for three weeks it was based on the River Waal near Nijmegen, with the Germans on the far bank.

marched on Kohima in the hills of Assam, an essential objective in their Operation 'U-Go' to invade eastern India.

The British 2nd Div will always be associated with the spring 1944 battles at Kohima and Imphal, which marked the turning point of the war in Burma, since it is that division's memorial that carries the poignant inscription *When you go home, tell of them of us and say, for your tomorrow we gave our today.* The division's 2 Recce Regt began by guarding 18 miles of the Dimapur–Kohima road with A Sqn, while RHQ and the other squadrons held a defensive 'box' at Zubza. In late April, HQ Squadron moved to Punjab Ridge and D Sqn to Lone Tree Hill; early May saw the regiment covering the southern flank at Jotsoma, 'sending out recce patrols, and mortaring enemy positions'.

The main mission for 2 Recce was to be as infantry, clearing the high, jungle-covered slopes of the Aradura Spur, which the Japanese had held since the early days of the fighting. First they had to force the enemy off Pulebadze Ridge; this operation began on 11 May, and eventually involved the entire regiment. On and about the Aradura Spur and the nearby GPT Ridge, Gen Sato had deployed a regiment – the equivalent of a British brigade – of his Japanese 31st Div supported by a mountain artillery battery. Although the Japanese battalions had suffered attrition by the time 2 Recce attacked, they were predictably ready to accept high casualties in the tenacious defence of their positions. The conditions in which 2 Recce fought were extreme, and their CO subsequently wrote that these caused him to revise all his previous ideas of time. Much reliance was placed on the local Naga hillmen as guides, since maps were hopelessly inaccurate, and supplies had to be carried by porters; the received wisdom was that it was impossible to carry out operations in this monsoon season. In a series of battles 2 Recce inflicted many casualties, but the Japanese made

During the Italian campaign, 4 Recce re-equipped its armoured car sections with the American T17E1 Staghound. With a top speed of 56mph and a road range of 450 miles, the Staghound mounted a 37mm main gun and co-axial and bow .30cal machine guns. However, its 13.7 ton loaded weight made it too heavy and cumbersome for the primitive roads of the Italian countryside, and it was more successful in NW Europe. (IWM KID 1268)

many aggressive counter-attacks. At the end of May the unit was ordered to withdraw to a position where it could more easily be resupplied; although this was only 2 miles distant, such was the terrain that it took about 20 hours to make the move. Although it had not taken the Aradura Spur, it had forced the Japanese to withdraw and 31st Div had been virtually destroyed.

It was autumn 1944 before 2 Recce was committed to an active part in the subsequent offensive by Gen Slim's Fourteenth Army, by which time D Sqn had been disbanded and a light recce regiment establishment adopted. For five weeks in January–February 1945 the regiment acted as a decoy force to convince the Japanese that an attack was to be made on the Sagaing Hills from the north. It later provided cover for an RAF airstrip at Sadaung by deploying Hookforce – C Sqn under Maj Hook, with A Coy of the Nepalese Mahundra Dal Regiment.

During the advance through Burma the unit's main difficulty was a shortage of vehicles, with carriers sufficient for only four carrier troops, while the number of scout cars fell to ten – enough for only two troops. 'The great deficiency was hitting power of a heavy nature. The lack of it was continually felt.' Among 2 Recce's actions was an encounter between Lt Tarmey's troop and some Japanese in which Cpl McAleer earned the MM; this troop had developed the tactic of driving into enemy positions 'with Brens firing, before dismounting and rolling grenades into Japanese bunkers'. In the course of several actions fought by Lt Sutton's troop, Sgt Rothwell gained the DCM. The regiment continued in its recce role as Fourteenth Army advanced to and beyond Mandalay, and sustained relatively few casualties given the amount of combat that it saw. On 7 April 1945, 2 Recce was withdrawn from the line, and before it could return the war had ended.

Chindits: 45 Recce

As is well known, MajGen Orde Wingate was authorized to follow his costly experimental long-range penetration behind Japanese lines in 1943 with another in March 1944 in much greater strength, with 9,000 men instead of a single brigade, and making much greater use of airpower for actual insertion as well as resupply. This Operation 'Thursday' was intended to disrupt enemy rear areas and communications in preparation for a general advance into Burma; in fact, shortly after it began the strategic picture was utterly changed by the Japanese offensive 'U-Go'.

Included in Wingate's force was 45 Recce, which had become part of 70th Div, now re-roled as long-range penetration groups. The brigades were divided into columns each of about 400 men, usually consisting of an infantry company of four platoons, a heavy weapons platoon with two MMGs, two 3 inch mortars and AT weapons, a 'commando' platoon for demolitions and booby-traps, a recce platoon with a section from the Burma Rifles attached, and RAF, sapper, signals and medical detachments.

Brigadier Bernard Fergusson, a veteran of the first Chindit expedition, commanded 16 Bde, to which 45 Recce was assigned. The regiment provided two columns, 45 and 54; the other units of the brigade included 51st/69th Field Regt RA fighting as infantry, 2nd Queen's Royal Regt and 2nd Leicestershire Regiment. Unlike the other

Soldiers of 2 Recce near Sadaung, Burma, plan their next patrol. These men wear a mixture of black berets with Recce badges and bush hats, with Indian-made jungle-green BD blouses and trousers. A jeep is visible in the background. (IWM SE 2236)

brigades, 16 Bde was to march into Burma rather than flying in. Their objective was a stronghold codenamed 'Aberdeen', which involved a 400-mile trek over unmapped mountains rising to 6,000 feet. They reached it two weeks behind schedule, due to a diversion to seize the Japanese outpost at Lonkin to assist Gen Stilwell's Chinese forces. From 'Aberdeen' 16 Bde were ordered to attack Indaw, and both recce columns were deployed on this operation. On 25 March, 45 Column met the enemy at Auktaw, forcing Japanese and Burma National Army troops out of the village at bayonet-point. Another encounter at Thetkegyin on the northern shores of Lake Indaw became known as the 'battle of the water bottles': seeking water supplies, 45 Column ran into determined opposition and suffered heavy losses, being obliged to withdraw after over two days' fighting. One machine-gunner, Tpr Matthew 'Paddy' Flynn, remained at 'his gun for forty-eight hours and stayed in position when the jungle around him was blazing, and the rubber pipe on his gun was melting with the heat'. Flynn was awarded the Military Medal; he later became the only member of the Reconnaissance Corps to receive a Bar to the MM.

Both 45 and 54 Columns later combined into a single column; after fighting off determined Japanese attacks on 'Aberdeen', 16 Bde was ordered to abandon the stronghold and return to India in May. In October, 45 Recce was disbanded as a Reconnaissance Corps unit to be re-formed as 2nd Bn South Staffordshire Regt, although some of its soldiers continued to wear the Recce badge.

The Arakan: 81 & 82 (West African) Recce

West Africa provided two divisions formed from the Royal West African Frontier Force (RWAFF) to fight in Burma, and each deployed recce regiments that formed part of the Corps. Both 81st and 82nd (West African) Divs fielded brigades representing the several West African colonies, and 81 and 82 Recce reflected this composition. The African soldiers proved to be excellent fighting men in Burma, in spite of having to fight on very light scales of equipment and with minimal support. Despite European perceptions they were not 'natural jungle fighters', since many were farm-workers or town-dwellers with no experience of forest conditions.

Their main area of operation was the Arakan on Burma's west coast, where 81 Recce was the first to go into action in January 1944 when a composite squadron was created to defend the Teknaf peninsula. The remainder of the regiment was assigned to defend Maungdaw and dominate the coastal plain of the West Mayu, for which purpose additional troops were placed under command. These soldiers were immortalized as 'the raiders of Arakan', and Gen Slim wrote that their raids were 'conspicuously successful'. It was one of 81 Recce's raids that identified the presence in Burma of the Japanese 55th Div which, until then, had been thought to be in the Pacific. At the end of March 1944 the regiment crossed the Ngakyedauk Pass into the Kalapanzin Valley, which it patrolled for the next month before rejoining its division.

Reorganized on a purely infantry basis, and with only '14 jeeps for commanders' recces', the regiment was to carry its own supplies 'on a headload basis'. Operations resumed in early October 1944; 81st Div was tasked with advancing down the Kaladan Valley to turn the

Japanese right flank, before moving to Paletwa where it would be relieved by 82nd (WA) Division. This involved 81 Recce in what was a Chindit operation in all but name. Harrying the enemy, the division made excellent progress; 81 Recce probed and patrolled to gather intelligence, and mounted diversions. The regiment even took to waterborne soldiering when, for two weeks, the captain of an LCT attached himself unofficially to 81 Recce – his vessel was very valuable for moving fighting patrols and carrying out other tasks. For fighting patrols use was also made of several impressed vessels, fitted with outboard motors dropped by the RAF. In January 1945, the two West

Gen Sir Oliver Leese, C-in-C Allied Land Forces SE Asia (ALFSEA), decorates a Recce NCO. The sergeant's badges of rank are worn as small white chevrons on shoulder strap slides rather than on his sleeves. (IWM SE 4035)

A group of highly decorated soldiers of 81 (West African) Recce; their division was formed in Nigeria but also recruited from the Gold Coast, Sierra Leone and Gambia. These men – from 5 Tp, A Sqn – include the recipients of a Military Cross, a Distinguished Conduct Medal, two Military Medals, three Mentions in Dispatches, and a Certificate for Gallantry. All wear KD battledress blouses and trousers, bush hats and 'ammo boots', with web belts and anklets apparently boot-polished black. The divisional sign of Ananse the clever spider is fixed temporarily to both upper sleeves of their blouses. (John Purdy)

African divisions took Myohaung in a pincer movement; after playing a significant role there, 81 Recce carried out mopping-up operations until, at the end of January, the division was withdrawn to India.

In the meantime 82 Recce, to which some 81 Recce personnel had transferred, was still in action. The regiment did not see the same intensity of operations as its sister unit, but was engaged in a series of minor actions, in one of which Sgt (later SSM) Isa Nupe earned the Military Medal. Throughout February, March and April 1945, 82 Recce harried the retreating Japanese until the regiment was withdrawn to monsoon quarters. Although some patrolling was carried out in May 1945, 82 Recce's active service was over.

SELECT BIBLIOGRAPHY

Brayley, Martin J. & Richard Ingram, *The World War II Tommy: British Army Uniforms European Theatre 1939–45* (Crowood Press, 1998)

Doherty, Richard, *Only The Enemy in Front (Every Other Beggar Behind…) The Recce Corps at War 1940–1946* (Tom Donovan Publishing, 1994)

Flint, Keith, *Airborne Armour: Tetrarch, Locust, Hamilcar and the 6th Airborne Armoured Reconnaissance Regiment 1938–50* (Helion & Co, 2004)

Howard, Roy, *Beaten Paths Are Safest. From D-Day to the Ardennes: Memories of 61st Reconnaissance Regiment, 50th (TT) Northumbrian Division* (Brewin Books, 2004)

Shilleto, Carl, *The Fighting Fifty-Second Recce: The 52nd (Lowland) Divisional Reconnaissance Regiment RAC in North-West Europe, September 1944–March 1946* (Eskdale Publishing, 2000)

Taylor, Jeremy, *This Band of Brothers. A History of The Reconnaissance Corps of the British Army* (White Swan Press, 1947)

PLATE COMMENTARIES

A: UNITED KINGDOM, 1941–42
A1: Second Lieutenant, 1941
When the Corps was formed no badge or other distinctions had been agreed, and the War Office considered various designs for several months. In the meantime, serving officers transferred to the Corps continued to wear the cap badge and buttons of the regiment into which they had been commissioned; in 51 Recce, officers from Scottish regiments were instructed to wear the headdress and badges of their parent units. Officers newly commissioned directly into the Corps wore the General List royal arms badge on a khaki field service cap. This officer, commissioned into the Corps, wears 1940 pattern 'economy' battledress with the Corps arm-of-service strip on both blouse sleeves; grass-green and lemon-yellow were selected for this, green always worn foremost, and green was adopted as the backing colour for officers' rank badges (see Plate H6).

A2: Corporal, 48 Recce, 1941
Among units transferring to the Corps was 5th Bn The Gloucestershire Regiment, which became the Recce battalion for 48th (South Midland) Division. This division became a 'lower establishment' formation in November 1941, and 48 Recce transferred to 43rd (Wessex) Div, becoming 43 Recce in January 1942. Other ranks also wore their original regimental distinctions, if any; this NCO wears the Glosters' coloured FS cap – a private purchase item, for wear off duty only – with regimental cap and back badges.

A3: RSM Harrison, RTC Lockerbie, 1942
Mr Harrison came to the Reconnaissance Training Centre from the Brigade of Guards; he maintained the Guards' superlative standards, and was described by one trainee as 'one of the straightest, most honest and soldierly men' that he had ever met. By 1942 the Corps had its badge and distinctions; RSM Harrison, who wears 1937 pattern BD with his warrant badge in bright metal on his forearms, has the Corps badge on his service dress cap, Corps' arm-of-service strips on his sleeves, and a lanyard in Corps colours.

B: NORTH AFRICA & ITALY, 1942–44
B1: Trooper, 51 (Highland) Recce; Egypt, October 1942
Divisional distinctions banned in Britain were permitted by Eighth Army's new commander, LtGen Montgomery, and when it arrived in Egypt in August 1942 this division restored its famous 'HD' sign, seen here on the shoulder strap slides of the khaki aertex shirt. All-silver cap badges were used by the three Scottish recce units; another distinction adopted by 51 Recce, from 8 September 1942, was a diamond-shaped Hunting Stewart flash (with the red line 'running upwards from back to front'), worn on the BD sleeves and on the left side of the steel helmet; the same tartan was also worn on the regiment's Tam o'Shanter bonnet as badge backing.

B2: Trooper, 46 Recce; Sangro river, Italy, October 1943
46 Recce was heavily engaged in conventional infantry combat following the Salerno landings, and the regiment's mortarmen saw considerable action. This soldier of a 2in mortar team, taken from a photograph, wears the khaki beret authorized for the Recce Corps and infantry Motor Battalions by ACI 2216 on 17 October 1942, with the brown plastic economy cap badge introduced in December 1941. The woollen pullover and serge BD trousers were welcome in the cooler weather of early autumn. His minimal 37 pattern webbing has the cartridge-carriers often issued to non-infantry troops in place of the basic pouches. He carries a triple-tube, six-bomb carrier; and his mortar has been modified by fixing what looks like a Bren carrying handle to the barrel's point of balance by means of a steel collar.

B3: LtCol K.G.F.Chavasse, DSO*, 56 Recce; Rome, summer 1944
At Termoli in southern Italy in October 1943, Kendal Chavasse became the only Recce Corps officer to earn a Bar (second award) to his DSO. The officers' bi-metal cap badge is worn on the green beret adopted for officers by this regiment, and retained even after the official change to the black Royal Armoured Corps beret for recce units in January 1944. On his khaki drill (KD) bush jacket he wears the ribbons of the DSO with Bar, 1939–43 Star and Africa Star, as well as the Mention in Despatches oakleaf on a khaki drab ribbon. His regiment was the recce unit for 78th Div, whose yellow-on-black battleaxe sign may be seen on the cloth tab looped to his shoulder strap and stud-fastened to his sleeve. Badges of rank are worn on temporary shoulder slides.

C: NORTH-WEST EUROPE, 1944–45
C1: Armoured car commander; Low Countries, winter 1944
Known as the 'pixie suit' or 'tank suit', this bulky oversuit was introduced for armour crews in 1943. Evolved from attempts to perfect a working garment that was comfortable, warm, waterproof and wearable inside an AFV, the suit could be worn over BD. It was made from heavy cotton, varying from an almost-pink shade to a definite buff, lined with angora shirt cloth, reinforced at knees, elbows and seat, and had a detachable hood and no less than 13 pockets. The shoulder straps were also reinforced, so they could be used to remove casualties from vehicles ('dead man's handles'). This car commander of a recce regiment also wears the Royal Armoured Corps steel helmet.

C2: Sergeant Millroy, DCM, 15 (Scottish) Recce, December 1944
Although several sources suggest that all personnel of 15th (Scottish) Div wore the Tam o'Shanter, photographs show that this was not always so in 15 Recce. When Sgt Millroy

The turret crew of a camouflage-painted Humber Mk IV display khaki berets, Recce right-shoulder lanyards, the early 'Reconnaissance Corps' shoulder titles authorized only in July–September 1942, and arm-of-service strips. The sergeant also wears a medium machine-gunner's white 'MG and wreath' skill-at-arms badge above his chevrons. (Tank Museum 2084/C1)

received the ribbon of his DCM from Field Marshal Montgomery in December 1944 he wore the black RAC beret, which had become official Reconnaissance Corps headgear from 1 January 1944. His cap badge is the white-metal Scottish version, but here without the 3in x 2in green backing adopted by this regiment. On his 1940 pattern BD he wears the 'Reconnaissance' shoulder title, 15th (Scottish) Div sign, Recce arm-of-service strip, and the 1939–43 Star ribbon.

C3: Trooper, Assault Troop, 3 Recce; France, Summer 1944

Every recce squadron deployed for infantry fighting an Assault Troop, which was well armed and equipped and highly mobile. Soldiers were carried in trucks or, later in the war, US half-tracks; each section had its own vehicle. This trooper of 3 Recce wears the new Mk III steel helmet with camouflage netting, 1940 pattern BD with Corps shoulder title removed, the sign of 3rd Div, and the Recce arm-of-service strip. He holds a Sten magazine loading tool.

C4: Lieutenant, 52 (Lowland) Recce, 1944–45

Among the regiments to adopt a cap badge backing was 52 (Lowland); here the silver Scottish variant badge is worn through a large green rectangle, on the officers' high quality version of the Tam o'Shanter. Other units that adopted a green cap badge backing were 15 (Scottish), 43 (Wessex), and 61 Recce. On the officer's sleeve may be seen the St Andrew's Cross of 52nd (Lowland) Div above the 'Mountain' title recalling the division's previous role. By 1944 the 1939–43 Star (later, 1939–45) service medal was being awarded to officers and men who had served in a previous campaign other than Africa. This subaltern is probably a 1940 BEF veteran of this or another formation.

D: VEHICLES
D1: Humber Mk III Light Reconnaissance Car, HQ 56 Recce; Sicily, August 1943

The Humber LRC, the 'trademark' of the Reconnaissance Corps, served with most regiments. This car of 56 Recce in Sicily is the CO's vehicle, and is painted across the front with the name 'Faugh A Ballagh' – the Gaelic motto of the Royal Irish Fusiliers, meaning 'Clear the Way!' For most of the war 56 Recce was commanded by LtCol Kendal Chavasse, a former Royal Irish Fusilier (see C3). When Gen Montgomery said that he wanted no more recce regiments in Eighth Army, 56 Recce was transferred from 56th (London) Div to the newly formed 78th Div, whose golden battleaxe sign may be seen on the left front mudguard; opposite this is the tactical serial of divisional recce units – '41' on a square halved green-over-blue. The car also bears the diamond symbol for HQ Squadron. Its faded camouflage, khaki-brown shade No.2, is a relic of earlier service in Tunisia, where European camouflage was more appropriate than desert sand.

D2: Humber Mk IV armoured car, 2 Troop, A Squadron, 53 (Welsh) Recce; Goch, February 1945

From the experience of 56 Recce in Tunisia it was quickly realized that the LRCs had to be supplemented with heavy armoured cars. The first such 'HAC' adopted was the Humber, which remained in service in different marks including the definitive Mk IV, the first British vehicle to mount an American 37mm main gun, together with a Besa 7.92mm machine gun; it had a reduced crew of three. This car, 'Laughing Boy III', was photographed firing its Besa at enemy positions near Goch in the Rhineland. The car is finished in what was now termed olive drab shade No.15. Armoured vehicles of this regiment carried a Welsh dragon symbol on the turret in yellow on dark blue. 'Laughing Boy III' appears to have a very faded black-on-yellow '7' bridging class marking painted on the right of the glacis, as well as an unusual repetition of the red A Sqn triangle and white 2 Tp number centred at the bottom. The divisional sign of 53rd (Welsh) Div on a dark green backing and the recce regiment's '41' are reversed from their usual positions on the front mudguards.

E: VEHICLES
E1: Humber MK IV armoured car; 3 Troop, D Squadron, 161 (Green Howards) Recce; Northern Ireland, April 1944

'Davenport', F117958, was commanded by Lt Allen. The regiment, re-roled from an RAC tank regiment, was unusual in having a fourth squadron; the yellow bar and white number '3' visible right of the driver's port on the front plate presumably identify D Sqn, 3 Troop. The white three-bar gate on an emerald background, the sign of Northern Ireland District (NID), adorns the nearside mudguard, opposite the usual recce unit '41'. (From a photo published in the *Northern Whig*)

E2: Daimler Mk I armoured car, A Squadron, 2nd Derbyshire Yeomanry, 51st (Highland) Division; Low Countries, autumn 1944

When 2nd Derbyshire Yeomanry joined 51st (Highland) Div as its recce unit in January 1944, after the division's original regiment was disbanded in Egypt, they adopted a Recce order of battle, with Humber LRCs and Daimler HACs. Personnel wore black RAC berets with Derbyshire Yeomanry cap badges. The vehicles bore Recce '41' and divisional 'HD' signs; the **inset** shows the unusual presentation on the rear of the turret box of a Daimler photographed while supporting infantry in 1944. The high rear markings may be because much crew impedimenta was stowed on the outside of the car, thereby obscuring the mudguards. The small yellow triangle denoting A Sqn is visible on the left side of the turret. The front of the right headlight housing seems to have been roughly painted

Early in the Italian campaign, 56 Recce was involved in the battle for Termoli. It was there that LtCol Kendal Chavasse, who commanded the defensive perimeter against German counter-attack, earned the Bar to his DSO (see Plate B3). He later commanded the Recce Training Centre, where this photograph was taken. Since he was then a full colonel he wore the staff badge on his service dress cap; and note the whistle and leather lanyard on the brace of his 'Sam Browne'. (LtCol H.K.P.Chavasse, MBE)

yellow for some reason. There is no visible bridging class mark, but for the Daimler this would have been '9' in black on the usual yellow disc.

F: AIRBORNE RECCE
F1: Jeep (Willys 5cwt 4x4 car), A Troop, 1st Airborne Reconnaissance Squadron; Oosterbeek, Holland, September 1944

The jeep proved ideal for airborne recce units, as it could be deployed by Horsa glider and carried a useful load. This jeep – captioned in an Arnhem photo as crewed by Tprs V.Taylor and A.Dickson of A Tp – carries a single .303in Vickers K-gun mounted on the right. The windshield has been removed, and the spare wheel moved to a mounting on the radiator (note on the retaining plate an indistinct triangular marking enclosing a two-digit number '2?'). Brackets and straps hold ammunition boxes on the bonnet, and a radio is mounted in the rear. A white star may be seen on the rear side, a narrow vertical yellow line as a centre-of-balance marking on the side, a medium-blue registration number along the side of the bonnet, and the usual '41' Recce serial on the right end of the bumper – both the latter are obscured here by stowed weapons and tools. Squadron personnel wore Airborne helmets, Denison smocks, Airborne BD trousers and basic 37 pattern webbing.

F2: Sergeant, 6th Airborne Armoured Recce; UK, spring 1944
Originally a Royal Armoured Corps squadron attached to 6th Abn Div, this became a regiment of the Reconnaissance Corps on 14 January 1944. Many original personnel continued wearing headgear and badges from their parent regiments, but new personnel, such as this NCO, wore the Recce badge – here the plastic version – on the maroon Airborne Forces beret. 'Reconnaissance' shoulder titles were sometimes used; however, this sergeant displays on his right BD sleeve only the parachute qualification brevet, above (on both sleeves) the Bellerophon-and-Pegasus sign and straight 'Airborne' title of Airborne Forces in light blue on maroon, above his badges of rank. No Recce arm-of-service strip was worn by this unit. Note the Airborne version of the BD trousers, with extra pockets including a large, chamois-lined expanding pocket on the left thigh.

F3: Major C.F.H.Gough, 1st Airborne Reconnaissance Squadron; Arnhem, September 1944
'Freddie' Gough – whose family had won three Victoria Crosses in previous wars – commanded 1st Air-Landing Recce Sqn in Italy in autumn 1943 before its transfer to the UK, where it became 'Airborne'. Major Gough, a Royal Navy veteran of the Great War, provided inspiring leadership in the desperate fighting at Arnhem; in this reconstruction from a photograph he is shown tired, dusty and not too recently shaved. He wears a Recce Corps badge embroidered in gold and silver thread on a maroon triangle sewn to the Airborne Forces beret; a camouflage net veil as a scarf over a light khaki shirt and tie; and a modified Denison smock with full-length zip, slanting chest pockets and knit cuffs, worn with a pair of corduroy slacks.

G: FAR EAST
G1: Trooper, 45 Recce; Poona, India, 1942–43
This regiment joined 70th Div (formerly 6th Div) after it was shipped from Syria to India in October 1942. Its LRC crews found the issue solar topee an awkward headdress, and modified it by replacing the front of the peak with an absorbent rubber 'bumper', of round section just over an inch in diameter, and rivetted in place. This trooper wears the modified topee with the regiment's flash of a yellow spear bisecting a 2in green diamond. No collar, shoulder or arm badges were worn on the khaki drill uniform.

G2: Bren gun No.1, 2 Recce; Kohima, Assam, May 1944
Fighting off the Japanese attacks around the vital bastion of

SSM R.D.Page of 61 Recce, the recce regiment of 50th (Northumbrian) Div, who earned the Distinguished Conduct Medal on 9 September 1944 at the Gheel Canal. The armoured cars of the regiment's C Sqn fought all day 'like tanks' to rescue cut-off infantry, though at the cost of heavy casualties. Just visible behind the badge on SgtMaj Page's black RAC beret is the green rectangular backing adopted by 61 Recce. (Author's collection)

Kohima in the jungle hills of the India/Burma border, 2nd Div needed every man they could put into the line in the infantry role. Operating on GPT Ridge south of the town, in support of the division's 4th Inf Bde, this trooper is indistinguishable from any other foot soldier, in felt bush hat, Indian-made jungle-green battledress blouse and trousers, and 37 pattern webbing equipment. As the gun No.1 he has its spares and tool wallet slung. Photos show men of the regiment wearing no insignia of any kind.

G3: Sergeant Isa Nupe, MM, 82 (West African) Recce; Burma, 1945
Sergeant Nupe earned the Military Medal in the Arakan in spring 1945; later, as a squadron sergeant-major, he was brought to London to take part in the Victory Parade. He

is shown as a sergeant, in Indian-made KD battledress blouse and trousers; interestingly, when portrayed in 1945 he still wore the khaki Reconnaissance Corps beret rather than the black RAC headgear. His rank chevrons are worn in plain white on the right sleeve; his medal ribbons are those of the MM, 1939–45 Star and Burma Star; and his divisional sign – crossed spears on a native porter's headband – is displayed on a hanging tab from his shoulder straps.

G4: Sign of 81 (West African) Division

The black spider on a yellow background was chosen by MajGen Woolner, the division's first GOC; it represents Ananse, a figure from Ashanti mythology who could change his guise and overcome foes by cunning instead of force. It was always worn pointing downwards, so that Ananse faced the enemy whenever soldiers aimed their weapons. (Ananse was not a tarantula, which is neither black, nor to be found in West Africa.)

H: INSIGNIA

H1: Reconnaissance Corps cap badge, yellow metal – other ranks.

H2: Corps badge, bi-metal, with gilt spear and nickel-plated lightning flashes and scroll – officers.

H3: Corps badge, variation in white metal – Scottish units.

H4: Inevitably, some units decided to modify their badges further, the principal examples being 15 (Scottish) and 49 (West Riding) Recce. The former adopted officers' service dress collar badges with the lion of Scotland on a yellow enamelled disc, all on a white O (the 15th letter of the alphabet).

H5: Coloured 'cap, field service' purchased by officers of 49 (West Riding) Recce – top, peak and curtain all Recce-green with lemon-yellow piping.

H5A: Officers of 49 Recce wore cap and collar badges with the white (silver) rose of Yorkshire added to the spearshaft.

H6: The Reconnaissance Corps arm-of-service strip – 2ins x $^{1}/_{4}$in, halved green and lemon-yellow, green always foremost; embroidered subaltern's rank 'pip' and field officer's king's crown, on green backings, as sewn to BD shoulder straps.

H7A: Original 'Reconnaissance Corps' shoulder title, authorized in July 1942. Only two months later authority for such distinctions was withdrawn throughout the Army on security grounds.

H7B: In June 1943, Army Order 905 restored the use of shoulder titles across the Home Army (supposedly after the intervention of Prime Minister Winston Churchill), and the Corps adopted one with the single word 'Reconnaissance'.

H8: Some battalions felt the need for more positive forms of identification. These included 4th Battalion, which adopted a flash worn on both sleeves, of a leaping black panther on a diagonally split background of yellow over green; this was designed by 2nd Lt E.M.Lyne, and was also used on battalion vehicles, again on a background of yellow over green. The sleeve flashes were made in handed pairs, the panther always pointing forwards. It was worn below the divisional sign but above the Corps strip.

Tpr A.Pearman, 15 (Scottish) Recce, photographed in early 1945 wearing the black RAC beret with silver Scottish badge, BD with open collar over a shirt and tie, Recce right-shoulder lanyard, 'Reconnaissance' shoulder title, 15th (Scottish) Div sign and Recce arm-of-service strip. Permission to wear ties and open collars, officer-fashion, had only recently been granted, and many soldiers added 'facings' to the BD collars by cutting off shirt tails; this accounts for a variety of shades. (Adrian Pearman)

H9: Standard vehicle tactical serial identifying the Recce unit within an infantry formation – white numbers on a square halved green-over-blue.

H10: Variation used by A Sqn, 43 Recce – black numbers on square divided diagonally, yellow-over-green.

H11: Arrangement of insignia on BD sleeve of a corporal wireless-operator, A Sqn, 43 Recce, 1944: Corps title; 43rd (Wessex) Div sign; arm-of-service strip; unofficial wireless operator's flash (fist and lightnings in buff, white and black on khaki) – non-regulation insignia were often adopted at unit level by British personnel; badges of rank. Note also that this regiment wore a green square badge backing on the khaki beret.

INDEX

Figures in **bold** refer to illustrations.